THE JOURNEY BEYOND ENLIGHTENMENT

THE NEXT STEP IN YOUR PERSONAL TRANSFORMATION

STUART WILDE

G&D MEDIA

Published 2023 by Gildan Media LLC
aka G&D Media
www.GandDmedia.com

FIRST EDITION 2023

Front cover design by David Rheinhardt of Pyrographx

Interior design by Meghan Day Healey of Story Horse, LLC

Library of Congress Cataloging-in-Publication Data is available upon
request

ISBN: 978-1-7225-0602-5

10   9   8   7   6   5   4   3   2   1

Contents

1

Why Seek Enlightenment?

Why would you need to go beyond enlightenment? And why would you bother to make this journey? I suppose the resounding reason is that if you look inside your soul, you'll see that there's something missing. You always know that there's something that isn't working, some bit that you don't know, that you haven't found, that you're wandering around looking for. Maybe you're looking for the key to everything, without knowing what the key looks like, or what it is that you're actually searching for.

Therefore, the reason for this journey beyond enlightenment is really to arrive at the complete you, the authentic you, the whole you.

Our human body is small—in measurement maybe five or six feet tall or slightly taller—but, in fact, deep down we are vast. We're bigger than the universe. Yet you are a microcosm. And then there's a macrocosm version of you that is absolutely enormous. The reason to make the journey and the reason to go into the unknown, and, of course, when you say unknown to people, they tend to get a little worried that you're going to be whizzing them off into some sort of totally chaotic place, but the journey into the unknown does take a certain amount of bravery.

But then this yearning, the nostalgia for eternity, is this thing we yearn to behold, and the journey beyond enlightenment is ego trip enlightenment. It's a spiritual elitism. It doesn't exist, but the journey beyond enlightenment is saying, *What I want is completeness. What I want is wholeness. What I want is to arrive back to where we all came from.*

One of the sacred cows of the New Age movement is the notion that the end goal of spiritual growth is enlightenment, or what some spiritual leaders call *living in the light.* To me, enlightenment is not the end goal, but just the beginning for the true spiritual adventurer. It's going ten feet under water in an ocean that is thousands of feet deep. There is a world of spiritual realities to be explored that are hardly even addressed or considered by the New Age mainstream.

In this book, I take you into the world of the etheric via your imagination, in order to explore a huge variety of new spiritual terrain: the morph, a spiritual overlay of energy that permeates our world, transdimensional beings, ESP, dematerialization, magical healing, bilocation, dimensions, and the existence of modern Camelots and much more. Beneath all of the wondrous realities, I explore one key essential truth: the only true spiritual path is a path that embraces the authentic you.

I'm going to show you something very empowering that is special yet usually misunderstood or hidden away. For the journey beyond enlightenment is essentially a journey beyond the confines of this three-dimensional reality, past what you think you know, to a hidden door inside a hyper-dimensional reality. There you'll see the true nature of the extraordinary power of what has come to be known as the authentic you.

Normally, we live in what might be a confined, rather fake humdrum existence with little inspiration as to the future, but I lay out how to step off that path, and I tell you how many people have literally walked into another world—a magnificent world of transdimensional beings and the potential of a super knowing that is not limited by force boundaries and damaging limitations of the ego and egocentric perceptions of life. There is a mirror world to this one, and I tell you the story of that and how to get there, and what to do to help yourself once you're there.

You decide how little or how much you feel you wish to explore. This book deals with the invisible you, the one you can't normally see. That is where your supernatural power is. It's akin to the Taoist concept of looking at the spaces between the leaves of a tree, rather than looking at the actual tree. It's all about what's in the gap and how you will learn to walk into that gap. Once you're there, looking back at the world, you will never see the world the same again. Much of the struggle and pain falls away, and you will see it all in a higher light.

The journey beyond enlightenment is not the acquiring of new rules. It's letting go of old rules and dogma to become more free, and it's not aligned much to the world of *yang*, which is the masculine force that conquers and prospers in a commercial world. It's more embracing of the feminine and prospering in the inner worlds, because so much healing comes from the feminine energy, which we call the feminine spirit or *yin*. The beauty of this spiritual journey is you *can* take as long as you wish, and go as far as you wish. Going just a little way allows you to formulate a new way of looking at things, and then you can come back to the path ten years later, if you wish.

People have been coming with me all the way starting about twenty years ago; they will probably still be there at the very end. Maybe it's because they know I'll get them there. It's fine to travel down the path a bit, and then take a detour to discover something about yourself. It's good not to be too dogmatic, and what works for you may not work for another.

Certain people, for example, are destined to become what I call the *fringe dwellers*. They're not necessarily hippie revolutionaries or New Age space cadets. The fringe dwellers are different in that they silently think differently. You might have been working at a humdrum tick-tock job at the post office for forty years, but in your mind, you don't belong to these systems. You know that you are a citizen of a far country, a spiritual consciousness that doesn't really fit the regular mindset of this world. Your thinking makes you different, not special, necessarily. It's just that you're not aligned to the way the world thinks.

Being on the fringe can sometimes cause you a lot of pain and difficulty, especially if you fight it. I realized I didn't fit at about the age of ten. I was raised in Africa before television was invented, and then I was shipped off to an austere English boarding school. It was like a prisoner of war camp. There I had to pretend to be an upper-crust Englishman, but the truth was I was neither upper crust nor English. I was a little African kid, albeit a white African kid. I knew nothing about the mindset or the ideals of an English gentleman and his pleasures, like rugby and cricket and other strange games and rituals I'd never seen before, but I knew which snakes were poisonous and which were not, but that wasn't very useful on the playing fields of England.

That's where my fringe dweller mentality started. At about the age of twelve, I formed a small alternative society at the boarding school. There were about a dozen of us. We lived in the roof of the school's gymnasium. It was a perilous journey across narrow iron girders to get to the gap between the gymnasium ceiling and the outside roof of the building. Once in our magical hidden world, we had to watch our step because if we missed the joist that held up the ceiling, we could fall through to the gymnasium floor twenty to thirty feet below.

I lived in that roof with my pals on and off for five years; every spare moment of my school life was in that roof. We never plotted to destroy the system, just to survive it. School was very nasty, a violent place, and we found if we stuck together, and if we pooled our resources, we could not only survive, but thrive. We got two shillings and sixpence pocket money each week, which at today's exchange rate is about twenty-four cents US, but with our capital we could buy stuff that other boys wanted such as candy and snacks and sell them at a small, but well-deserved profit, and so our little society of teenage fringe dwellers thrived.

We felt free and safe living in the roof away from the school prefects and masters and teachers who would beat us with a stick at the slightest excuse, and we were quick and agile and fairly fearless. We could run across the narrow iron girders that held up the roof in seconds, even in the dark. We never got caught, not once in five years. The interesting thing was that the boy who lived in the roof was the authentic me, the feeling me, the sensitive me, the one who would share and help others, while the boy who was on the playing fields pretending to be an English gentleman was the fake competitive me, an image that was forced upon me against my will.

We all suffer from conformity. It's a mind control disease. It's how society and our families legislate over us to keep us in their mental prisons. It's ghoulish really. In my twenties, my mother, who was a great believer in spiritualism and mediumship, gave me a book called something like *The Powers that Be*. It was all about spiritualism and the hierarchies of angels that guide spiritual seekers to a higher perception.

I suddenly saw there was a possible way out of this harsh world, to a spiritual world, a place for those who didn't fit. It was another ceiling to discover and perhaps hide behind. To know that that was a possibility changed my life. It was an enormous impetus for me. I suddenly saw being a fringe dweller was just fine as long as you're not plotting to burn down city hall. It's fine not to fit; it's fine to seek the society of others who also don't fit. It's fine to travel away and leave it all behind you and embark on a great journey of discovery and a voyage to find the freedom of the real you. It's okay and permitted to find your own relationship with God rather than borrowing one from others, or having one imposed upon you by some system of control or an institution.

I soon made it my life's quest to find the hidden door—the one that leads to the celestial worlds—and after about thirty years of trial and error and a few spooky dead ends, I finally found it and so will you if you have a desire for it.

What Is Your True Identity?

The Journey Beyond Enlightenment is essentially the journey beyond the ego's fears and its incessant demands and the stress that pursuit creates in your life. Fear is a part of the ego's prism; it drives you to act strangely. You can change that. The world of the ego is not an authentic world.

What we seek to do in our journey beyond enlightenment is to arrive back at the authentic self, the feeling self. That is your true identity. It is the eternal you and in it is the part of the knowing of who you are and what your life's mission is.

Who are you? What are you doing here? What purpose do you serve? Once you can answer that, you disappear, well sort of. It's as if everything you think you are, your personality, and all that you know and hold dear, your life story, the very memory of you melts and disappears, and at the very end of the journey, there is nothing there, just an eternal silence. Nothing. Just an indescribable beauty.

The journey sounds strange, eerie even, but, in fact, it's very beautiful because once you go past all the definitions of yourself, then you will also go past the pain, and you will eventually know who you are and what your life's mission is. You will see yourself beyond terms of enlightenment, beyond the arrogance of ignorance, and you'll finally know the secret, which will bring you great joy.

In later chapters here, I discuss at length the resonance of your soul, your sound, an imprint that you make on life. That imprint of your soul can heal not only you and your loved ones, but humanity in general; and you won't necessarily have to hang a shingle on your door, advertising your opening hours, as that may be too limiting. If your resonance is right, you will only have to walk past people and they will already begin to heal. To change your resonance is to change the resonance of the world.

We define what we think we are, and that makes us feel safe. To that end, we work hard to become Harry the

Doctor or Mrs. So & So, the mother, the social worker, the teacher, These are evolutions of the mind and the intellect, but it can be a tiring and limiting experience playing out the role you have selected for yourself, which is often the recipe for a lot of pain because your whole existence is framed in the definitions you and others have invented for yourself. They are emotional, intellectual clusters that you belong to, groupings of like-minded people, much like joining a golf club, and being in the energy and cluster of golf, and in the mind-set of golf.

In the end, you are vast and eternal, and all the silly rules and limitations will eventually melt and become meaningless and unimportant. For you are destined to arrive at the infinite you. You enter into the eternity of all things where human titles and stuff, even the human body, have no meaning.

It's in the losing of the *you* that you think is you that you eventually arrive at the *new you*, that disappeared identity. The human who had so much fear and pain is represented by a vast version of you connected to every-thing. Apart from all the primal forces and the spirits of nature and angelic beings and all manner of wonder-fulness that exists beyond the memory of what I call *stored pain*—which are the ancient memories in your subconscious or your soul—the connection you make is one of pure bliss. All the honor and reconciliation of that is beyond the light and the dark, beyond solid and not solid. It is a fusion of your soul, a deliverance from evil, a place where you hover as nothing and everything at the same time.

It's a quirky thing to think of, but once you let go of what you think you are, and the definition is that you are, then you can become everything. It's the bliss of belonging, once more the bliss of remembering.

The Illusion of the Ivory Tower of the Ego

Let's talk about how to go from phony to authentic, and how you will turn your evolution to go the other way. For that will power you along, and you need that flip of perception before we can access anything else. Imagine it like this: Life for many is confusing and scary and rather brutal at times. It's a painful journey through the unknown. You have to struggle and compete and work hard to make ends meet.

The ego soon builds a tower for you to live in. It feels safer there. The tower protects you from dealing with people and experiencing pain and disappointment. You're elevated in your mind, anyway, above the crowd. From there you can gaze down on humanity through your separation and your imagined specialness, and you could sell yourself the idea that the destiny of ordinary people is not your destiny, that you've been elevated and chosen and made special. That is why the ego likes to be higher in distance from others. That is why the ego likes observers and glamour.

Observers make the ivory tower of the ego more real, and that is why people boast and often make a great story of their minor achievements. They seek recognition and status; they seek altitude for their ivory tower. The ivory tower is sustained by the electricity of the ego. The more electricity a person has, the more they can be moody, capricious, and self-centered. The moody demanding pop star is an example of the electricity of the ego running rampant.

To sustain the power of their importance and their divine-like status, they need constant attention, constant input; it's a high-maintenance lifestyle. The ego drives people to seek that status and a position over others. Glitzy stuff, flashy cars, the red carpet, the VIP lounge, all create attention. The attention of others creates electricity for the ego, and through that incoming energy, the ego seeks to falsely elevate itself. It's our ego's way of raising itself up to the center stage.

We seek electricity, external energy sources, to hold us up. It helps us feel safe and less vulnerable. That is the illusion of specialness that comes from the ego's sense of separation, but that specialness often comes at a terrible price. For in the isolation of elitism and the ivory tower, you become ever so slightly mad.

The electricity of the tower fries you in the end, as you will need more and more and more to keep the illusion going. It blinds you to reason; you only see your mind and your ideals and your terms and definitions. The other six billion people here on Earth are more or less irrelevant, except as how they might feed the ego's needs—you on top of the tower with an old rusty gun, marching up and down guarding the edifice of your ideals. It doesn't really matter if your ideals are tiring you out, or if they're gradually killing you, as long as you're a king or queen of the tower and as long as you can shut out pollution in the form of contradictions of the ego and the presence of other humans and other ideas.

Of course, at the top of the tower, the madman or the madwoman isn't actually any safer than anyone else. The height is an illusion, and the protection is arbitrary at the very least. The reason is that the tower costs time and money and stress to maintain. You have to buy a car that is perhaps more than you can afford. Maybe you live in a place that costs too much rent that has trappings that have to be financed, and the ego will want this and that and then another thing, and soon you are its slave rushing about trying to give it what it wants, and it usually wants one thing after the next.

Take a moment and take a good look. What is your ivory tower made of? Are you a prisoner of stress and your ideals? Are you spiritually trapped? And being up there can make you lonely and isolated, and usually you'll be very cold spiritually, even though you may pretend to be social and warm while in fact you see everyone as dispensable, and perhaps you treat them with disdain and indifference.

Your ego acts as the ministry of authorized information. It's up in its madhouse, and anyone contradicting the edicts of the minister of information is due for annihilation, or you'll banish them from your world and send them away. People who contradict information you hold to be true have to be made wrong and belittled. This is the controlling mechanism of the dark side of mankind. It's our attempt to impose ourselves on others. We know best. We are the divinely selected ones, the chosen ones. All others must be heretics and heathens because they don't agree with us, and, of course, they are not quite as special and chosen as the fool on the tower, for he or she is divinely selected to be something very important and very special.

Most religions and most spiritual groups and philosophies create the sense of the enlightened being, as being a superior being; here are the ignorant people and here is the enlightened buddha on the path who has the answer, and so on.

It's this idea of, let's say, the Pope is infallible, that this buddha over here is enlightened, and, of course, these are elitist concepts. There are concepts that seek to raise a human above others, so we must worship his being and kiss his toe because he's enlightened. That's the old-fashioned way of looking at enlightenment, but the way that we deal with enlightenment here is to understand that enlightenment is a trap.

The minute you sit at the crossroads and you're enlightened, then you need a phone and a cushion and cellos around, and your students. You need to create an ashram for the world of the demigod. You're some grand bishop or cardinal, and you have a throne and robes and a gold chalice to drink from, and all of that is a construct of ego. It's a construct of control where these priests and these enlightened beings will establish control over the lesser mortals in the congregation.

I see enlightenment as basically a con—a place to get stuck. If you're stuck as an enlightened being, you haven't got anywhere to go. You just create this ashram around you, and enlightenment is utterly worthless to you. Because we seek to retreat, we seek to go sideways, we seek to become nothing; if you had all the power in the world, and you could literally materialize things out of nowhere, you couldn't show it to people. Because if you did, you would become like a magician on TV. You would have followers and worshipers and would be controlling the people by your power and their lack of power.

That's why all power is hidden away, all true knowledge is hidden, and the only knowledge that's available is the fake knowledge.

You read documents, you read dogma, and they seek to entrap you, to take you away from where you find yourself. The society and the ideas that you were born with are those that you feel comfortable with, and they seek to impose another set of rules, and those rules almost always involve subjugating yourself to them, to the meditation group, to the church, to the ashram, to whatever it is. They're all basically forms of entrapment.

What we seek to do is to become "unentrapped," so to speak. We seek to say, *Look, this enlightenment thing is a crock, because I don't want to sit on a throne and have hundreds of followers. What I just want to do is have the knowledge and the power. I do understand that once I have the knowledge and the power, I'll not be able to show it to anybody, but that doesn't bother me because in my heart, I want to serve humanity. I don't have to be aware of the fact that they are aware or not aware.*

It's like the idea that the initiate can walk through a village, change its evolution, bring calm to the village, because the initiate's heart is resonating at such a pulse that the imprint the initiate puts on the village calms everybody and wakes them up and makes them more aware. Then the initiate walks out of the village, and they never did figure out who she was or he was. He just stood at the well for a day or two and talked to a few people, and that was all. That's the idea that we're coming to, that the true power is always hidden, and true knowledge is not available. The only knowledge that's available, generally, is the lies.

Spiritual Enlightenment Empowers You

Are you familiar with the work of Masaru Emoto, the Japanese professor who has photographed frozen water crystals? In his 2004 book, *The Hidden Messages in Water*, he hypothesized that water could react to thoughts, whether positive or negative. He would hold a tube of water and write on it the word "Hitler," and then he'd freeze the water and take photographs of the water crystals, and they would come out all dark and chaotic. If he wrote the word "joy" on the label, the water crystals formed like beautiful snowflakes.

Professor Emoto's pioneering work really highlights for us the effect you have on your surroundings, and the way you imprint light for the better or for the worse. Almost all of your body is water. So you're a mobile puddle that travels around with you warping reality, or

healing it, depending on how you feel and express yourself minute by minute.

The water crystal of what you are is important.
When you're warm and tactile and you genuinely care for
humanity from your heart, you push away the imprint
of negative dark beings, and you draw to you the begin-
nings of a celestial dimension, and heaven on earth walks
around with you. When you're cold and you seek domination and control over others or you seek vengeance or you
wish others ill, you fall into the arms of the darker forces.
It's easy to do. We all fall the other way at some point in
our lives as the ego likes power, and it seeks vengeance
and an eye for an eye and a tooth for a tooth.

All sounds pleasing to the ego, but that is the love-
less world of the phony self. There you can find justifica-
tion for all sorts of nastiness and silent crimes against
humanity. It takes a brave person to go the other way
and offer forgiveness instead of seeking vengeance.

You may think that salvation comes from being special and chosen and part of some elite system. Dream
on. Elitism is very dark, as it excludes others. In fact,
deliverance comes from ordinary humans and not
needing to be special. Drop being special and you're
already walking in the right direction. Part of the
reverse perception I speak of is hard to see for we're
all programmed to seek satisfaction and to seek the
attention of others. Yet the right direction is to seek to

become humble and sensitive toward others, and rather than asking how will life sustain you, you should start to think of how you might serve humanity. Spiritual empowerment in that journey beyond enlightenment doesn't seek to make you more special. In fact, it seeks to liberate you from the need to be special. It liberates you from the need to hold up the ivory tower, and the need for more and more.

When you watch TV, you'll see one guy who claims he is the world's greatest crocodile catcher. Then another fool claims he's the world's greatest bounty hunter, and another is the greatest running back and she is the greatest chef and there there's a whole host of the world's greatest rappers, hip hoppers and flip floppers making incredible baskets on the basketball court. In the end, they're all mad fools on the ivory tower, calling out to the heavens saying, *I am the greatest, the king and queen of the castle. I'm squeaky clean and special and different, and I'll be forever immortalized in my deeds. I am selected by God and I am special. That is what I am.*

Imagine if you didn't have to be special, how weird that might feel for some. Maybe it would feel really liberating. People could ask if you are the world's greatest blah, blah, blah, and you'd say proudly, *No, I'm not the world's greatest anything.*

I work terribly hard to arrive last. The trick is to arrive eventually at nothing and not be the world's greatest anything. I've learned a very simple secret, and that is to retreat from the world of boasting and to step back into silence and the comfort of the forest. I found it best to let all those on the ivory tower push and shove and compete while I stand off and watch. I feel safe because I'm not sticking out in the crowd ready to be knocked off by another competing ego, and I'm not in the competition of humanity at all. The trick is to agree to lose. You don't have to win. Agree to be last, be happy with last.

People might ask if you are bothered that you have to wait in line while other important people in front of you go ahead, and you will say, *No, it doesn't bother me where I am in the line.* The people that need to strive and push and fight to go first will burn themselves out and become sad, and while they may be first in today's line, tomorrow they won't have a place in any line and that might upset them. I'm happy to take whatever place in the line no one else wants, because my place in the line is irrelevant, as I'm busy watching a sparrow talking to another on the roof over there.

Now here's a reverse idea that's quite exciting that might impel you to a new perspective. What if I told you that you could easily become one of the most powerful people in the world, and that you could have vast energy, so vast that you could get almost anything you wanted just by deciding to materialize it in front of your very eyes? But there are a few catches. First you can never tell anyone that you have the power, and you can never do anything in front of people that might give them that idea, or any showing off like that. In fact, to make it work, to keep to your agreement, you will actually have to be anonymous about it all, and sometimes you will purposely try to look like a bit of a fool and a bit of an incompetent so that people never think that you know what you know. The next catch is that you can have anything you want almost immediately because you can materialize it, but because you have that power, you will never be able to use it.

The reason why you can't is this: You're here to work and love and understand the Earth plane. You're here to transfer energy to others. That's it. You can't use your power to enhance your ego and become the world's greatest something or other. You can keep bits of it and make your life easy and flowing, but you can't hoard the power; you have to get rid of it as it comes into your life. Otherwise, you'd be misusing the power just as everybody else tries to misuse it.

If you're serious about going beyond enlightenment, what you're saying is you will work silently to become enlightened. You will never tell a soul once you make it. Almost all the initiates I know—the ones who have a real command of the hidden door—are humble and quite anonymous. You would never spot them in a crowd. They don't have to say much because they do know. You're going to go beyond enlightenment because you don't need enlightenment. It's a trap for the spiritually elevated. You probably knew that, but maybe you needed me to remind you. The fact is the more inner power you have, the less you will ever be able to show anyone.

Then you may ask, *What is the point of striving to acquire perception and abilities if I can never show anyone or make a profit from it?* Here's what I learned going down that way: All great power is always hidden. It can pass through the night and rescue people from their ivory towers, from their tormented lives, and to love and serve humanity to a better end. That is it. In rescuing people you'll have more than anything else in the world. People will be pulled to you endlessly. It's an etheric thing. It's in your life force energy; you can help people without their knowing, without their ever having realized that you helped them.

Silent Service to Humanity

The opposite of accumulation and egocentricity is humility and service. Let's go back to the reverse. At some point, you will have to learn to serve humanity if you have not already done so. You can't get out of this evolution and go beyond it without first having served. At the end of your life, all the things that you ever did for yourself count as nothing. They have little or no value. The great empires you won, and the battles you fought with others, and all the striving will be worthless.

There's only one currency of worth that you can take with you, and that is what you felt about humanity. What did you do for them? Did you love them and care for them? Did you go out of your way to make sure they were okay? Did you give them what you had? Did you share? Or did you hoard? Did you run to eat first? Or did you eat last? Nothing else counts.

All the other ivory tower stuff and empire building and triumph over others was just fluff. It showed how easily tricked you could become, and all the anger and hatefulness was just one ivory tower clanging as it fell against others.

So what have you done for others? That's the only question you will have to answer. If your karma is good, the question will be easy. You will humbly turn and wave your arm all around, and there will be those that you have healed and those that you held in your arms when they were scared, and those that you provided for when they fell into misfortune. There might be thousands of them, maybe tens of thousands. It's unconditional love, without having to get something back or expecting anything in particular.

Action Step: Do this sometime in the next week or so. Do something valuable for someone without their knowing that you did it. Never mention your deed to anyone, and you'll soon get what I'm speaking of.

There are people out there that you haven't met yet who can't manage without you. They are like wounded children. They were given the wrong set of coordinates. Their life is bound to failure and misery, and what little meaning they have can be stripped from them in a second. Their cells will become polluted by their darkness, and the slippery path to the end is in sight. They have no hope. None. They will die surrounded by their ideals, surrounded by ugliness, surrounded by the dark forces, and only you can save them—if they want to come, that is.

Remember, you can't be of service if you feel obligated to do so through shame, guilt, and duty or if your ego needs the lightness of it all. Not if you think, *Look at me, how marvelous I am; I'm serving humanity.*

Service is a silent act that comes from a deep inner connection to the souls of other humans and the well-being of the animal kingdom. You serve because it's your destiny to do so and you want to. It's a form of deliverance, and in delivering your own soul to a spiritual redemption, you also deliver others and they will become your passport to the hidden doorway I've spoken of. It's all in the feeling of your humanity and in the expressing of it, how large your heart can become. In that, they will come to see the hidden door within you.

To be able to go into another world and see the celestial nature of it all, you have to cross a dark world to get there. I'll talk about the morph and the mirror world in the next chapter. I think you'll find it very exciting and unusual, but first you have to look and see if you have a genuine spirituality inside you. Do you just pretend to be nice? Sometimes the living-in-the-light approach—that sort of New Age people espouse—is sweet, but it isn't authentic because it makes you into a suffering servant, or it causes you more pain than necessary.

You aren't required to suffer other people's pain for them, but you are required, if you want a healthy lifestyle, to set boundaries. You can say to somebody, *Listen, I truly love you and adore you, but when you play the trumpet at three in the morning, it's bloody irritating, because I have to go to work at five. Please stop or move out.* It's always to do with communication, being there for them as a human, not criticizing them and making them wrong because they play the trumpet, but laying a boundary that says, *Look, if you want to play the trumpet, you're going have to move out, brother. I know you're only seven years old, but you'll have to figure it out. You got to listen to what Daddy says and you ain't playing the trumpet at three a.m. At the point when you can manage on your own, that's fine. Or maybe we can come to a mid-*

dle ground and we can get a trailer for you at the end of the yard, four miles away, and you can go play there.

Again, living in the light doesn't require an approach where you let the world trash you and ride roughshod over your feelings. It's always about being authentic and true to people.

Therefore, when something is driving you nuts, you can say so, but, of course, what happens is we make the mistake of coming out from a vindictive critical approach. We're saying we are squeaky clean and want to sleep but someone is jolly dark for playing the trumpet. The person is not dark for playing the trumpet, however. They love the trumpet, and maybe your staying up all night, not sleeping is fine by them. They're not evil because they play the trumpet.

The main approach is one of not making people dark, just accepting who they are, and allowing them to be who they are, and then setting a boundary when what they are doing is detrimental or irritating or difficult for you.

Anytime that you're showing your spirituality, you're in the shadow; whereas, the more squeaky clean and innocent you pretend to be, the more dark you actually are. That's your darkest moment when you proclaim how wonderful you are. It's the healer that makes this great show of healing, or the guru that makes a great show of being wise, or the teacher who has this massive hall and 7,000 people come and touch her leg or something. That's a big load of ivory tower.

Again, I'm talking about humility. If you heal, you heal without anyone knowing that you've healed them. If you teach, you teach without ever realizing that you taught because you taught by example, and that's the genuine healer. The genuine healer is one who doesn't realize they've healed you. Or they've healed you very inconsequentially. They've sort of made a passing remark, and suddenly that passing remark clicks into your psychology and you realize that the whole of your sickness comes from the fact that your relationship with your brother is toxic. So they healed you, in that way.

We all have to go through the sort of arrogance of enlightenment. We all go through elitism to work out how terrible it is. Some people never work it out, and they go to their grave in this sort of elitist mindset. With enlightenment for many people, there's this sort of spirituality that they'll walk around with—a great sort of thing on their chest—the medallion that people sort of stuff that expresses their spirituality, but that isn't spirituality. The idea is to be spiritual without anyone ever realizing you are spiritual.

We go from being completely egocentric and unaware, to being much more aware, and then we all go through the elitism of spirituality, believing that we've been chosen, which, of course, is one of the crimes of the fallen angel—to be like a god. We seek to become as a god, higher than ordinary people, and at the other end of it, we realize we didn't need enlightenment in life, and it was a pain in the neck, so we burn all the robes and all those gongs and all of that stuff, and then we walk out and infiltrate back into society without anybody ever figuring out who we are.

The Greatest Gift: Redeem Yourself

In my book *Affirmations: How to Expand Your Personal Power and Take Back Control of Your Life*, I talk about a concept called *variance*, which speaks to the essence of a positive reversal of self. Variance is the gap between what you pretend to be, what you think you are, the mask or persona that you present to the world, and what you *actually* are. You could say that variance is a tape that measures the height of your ivory tower.

All great spiritual journeys and the path of the initiate lead toward an ego death—a place where you become aware of the variance—and then the tower falls in front of your eyes. The authentic you has enormous power, and when you join it and become the same as it, a synapse of energy takes place. It's a burst of light caused by a sudden fluctuation in the quantum field.

This is vital to your enlightenment. If you don't collapse the illusion voluntarily, it is eventually collapsed for you. If you can control the collapse gradually, it's much less painful than when it comes upon you in a fast hurry imposed from elsewhere. Let me explain.

The reason why people feel blank and hopeless and in despair is because they don't have the power of their own soul to drive them along. It is as if the real you is locked away and held prisoner in the tower by the phony you. I don't know if you've ever felt that there was something terribly wrong, something missing in your life, a splinter in your mind as Morpheus says in *The Matrix*, a film. The missing bit is in the mirror world. There's another you, the feeling you, that is formed by the subconscious mind. It is the storehouse of your dreams. It is the authentic you. It is the perpetual memory of you, your soul.

Once you come back and retrieve the authentic you, suddenly all sorts of creativity and possibilities come from within you, and you have the opportunity to garner real worth in your life. Sure, that might be a nice money-making idea. Or it could just be newfound friendships and a sense of belonging.

Abundance is not necessarily in the form of cash. It's the warmth of humanity and animals around you, it's service to mankind, and it is being served. We are driven by fear, inadequacy, bad luck, and poor choices.

We are driven by many factors. This is not a level playing field, so you should not be too hard on yourself and others.

Action Step: Get a little notebook that you can slip into your purse or your pocket and start, over the next few days, to jot down all the things in your life that make sense, and the ones that don't. You are looking to notice the variance between what you have to do and what you really feel about it. Some of it will be obvious and you'll know it's phony, and some of it is more obscure. It'll only dawn on you as you think about it and as you ask for your super knowing to show you.

You have to be fair with yourself and compassionate. You can't cheat on yourself or tell yourself lies, as that is a variance of its own, isn't it?

Draw a line down the center of your little variance booklet, and put **true** on the one side of the center line and **not true** or **partly true** on the other.

- Your job or business, do you like it? Are you fulfilled? Or do you hate it?
- Home, is it fulfilling and supportive or is it a nightmare? Is it where you want to be? Can you afford it?
- Relationships, are they supportive or draining?
- Money, are you sensible and honest or irrational and dishonest?

- Lifestyle, is it healthy and sustaining or unhealthy and destructive? If it's destructive, it's probably your inner shadow trying to kill you. Are you brave enough to look at that and set yourself free? Or will you remain a victim? Can you love yourself, lumps and bumps and all?
- Time management, are you rushing about with very little time for yourself? That is a variance of its own, one that you should look at.

Then you look at if you really care about delivering your soul to a new redemption. Perhaps it doesn't really bother you. Perhaps you feel you're already perfect. Such thoughts are a trap. Remember that and then ask how you relate to others.

- Are you distanced from humanity? Do you really care for them? Is it all about you and what you want in this lifetime? Or are you aligned to the needs of others?
- How much love do you offer and how much silent resentment and hate? Are you an angel in disguise or a hidden predator? Are you stingy or generous?
- Are you open and accepting or closed down and dogmatic? Do you cast a kind eye to everyone? Do you exhibit a deep sense of justice and acceptance, live and let live, or are you judgmental and cruel toward others?

The way to work this out is this: Think about someone you don't really agree with. Then ask yourself if you respect them anyway. Do you care for their humanity even if you don't like them? Do you care for their soul, even if you virulently disagree with their opinions and their actions in life?

This type of equanimity is vital because, in the mirror world, any kind of judgment or antagonism will soon take your spirit down. It's a bad trait to find fault in others and to denigrate them and make them wrong.

You eventually want your life to be seen as proper and right. How will you do that if you don't offer that to others? If you've always made them wrong? Taking an equitable stance toward humanity is the only safe way to go across to the mirror world.

Finally, here in this opening discussion on reversal, can I ask you a really difficult question? Are you grateful? I mean, truly grateful? Or do you just pretend? When you say *thank you* do you mean it from your heart? Or is it just a social thing fobbing people off? Are you actually relating to someone's soul, and acknowledging them for their work and their kindness to you?

I ask because I've noticed that much of the time people are not grateful at all, and they don't even bother to say *thank you* properly. They just expect to be sustained, but they can't acknowledge the goodness that's come to them from others. Sometimes I think they feel that they're owed a living in this life, regardless of how little effort they put in.

Gratitude is important. It goes hand-in-hand with humility and softness. Do you see how spooky and wonderful it gets real quick, if you do this right? It'll make you cry, because you will see the darkness of it all, and once you see it, and once you own it, your life will dramatically change, I promise. I've seen thousands of people go through this, and some of it brought tears and compassion and moments of heaving emotion, but at the end, they came out light and angelic and forgiven and liberated.

The greatest gift you can offer yourself in this life is to redeem yourself. Once you agree to stop running away from yourself, you will be free and then you'll be able to see it properly. I've never seen instant absolution, instant redemption, however. All there ever was could be described as a gradual climbing out of a dark world of variance and confusion and fake ideas toward the spiritual, authentic world. You don't need to beat yourself up. It's okay to screw up—that was your karma and other people's karma—but you just have to look and see and accept all those aspects of who you are, the nice bits and the horrid bits.

Let's review a few more ideas of reversal. Life can be scary; that can cause fear. The natural reaction is to become more aggressive and more yang toward others, but eventual safety and a higher perception lies in the power of softness or yin. Some know this already, but you may not always embrace it. It isn't obvious at first, but the ego feels that the more threat it offers, the safer it will be, but that's not so. It doesn't seem obvious at first, yet the more aggressive you are, the more the hard forces come against you.

Make Peace with the World

Spirituality is a measure of how soft you can become, not what rules you follow. It seems strange but in establishing a spiritual softness, you come to the first of three liberations. Each is an emotional release and a huge spiritual advance. At the end of this chapter, I provide a guided meditation. It's a quiet session of prayer and introspection. You will be taken to the three liberations, so you can go there any time and work on them and process them more and more. They're vital, but you cannot proceed without them. The energy of the world is rapidly shifting. Your life will become ever more problematic without these perceptions.

In the first liberation you have to agree to make peace with the world. What I've discussed so far is an unobtrusive attempt for you to make peace with yourself, to turn yourself around and go the other way. Now you have to go beyond the story of your life and evolve beyond it. That is the enlightened way.

For some people, to learn to forgive themselves is difficult, but again, it's because they make such a story of everything. I know people who have gone into inner-child therapy who, ten years later, they're grown forty-year-old millionaires, and some of them are still whingeing on about their inner child and their mother was inadequate and their father was a drunk.

Let it go. Let it go.

You have to go into an act of contrition to observe the mistakes you made. You know where you genuinely feel sorry, you don't just fob it all off with that by saying, *Well, sorry about that.* You feel sorry and then you go into atonement, and atonement is where you attempt to make good with the people that you've hurt, but if you can't, because they don't live here anymore, so to speak, then you atone by being kind to other people.

So the first act is awareness. The second is attrition. The third is atonement, and then beyond that it's transcendence.

In other words, you're not callous; you're not shrugging and saying, *Oh, well, that's it.* You completely comprehend where you made mistakes. And you're sort of embarrassed about the fact you did make those mistakes, but in the higher knowing in the sort of super knowing, you understand, you are weak.

Today, affirm that you won't make the same mistakes again, or if you do make the same mistakes, try to make smaller ones. You understand that when you made those mistakes, you really damaged other people, you hurt their feelings, and you feel sorry for the fact you hurt them. You don't want to hurt them; you want to raise them up.

Attempt to atone in whatever way you can atone, and then you transcend by reviewing it properly, atoning as best you can, creating this act of contrition, which is the act of saying to yourself, *Look, I'm not going to do this again; I realize I've really hurt people here.* And then allow yourself time to just walk beyond it or go beyond to higher and better things, which kicks into the idea of service. How will you serve, because in service, we atone for the crimes of our past? It involves making peace with humanity.

You can understand if you are emotionally involved in running battles with others, and you harbor resentments. You are perpetually linked to them as if you are spiritually welded to the people that you hate or fight with or resent, and they will probably have a very low spiritual energy, as they may be abusers or predators or aggressive and or arrogant. You can't rise above them until you release them and let them go.

In the mirror world, which is the world of feelings and impulses and sentiments, you cannot escape from anyone that you are mentally or emotionally engaged with or any group of people that you focus on with your mind, and/or with resentments or negative emotions. You and they exist in the same place in the mirror world. Imagine it as a neighborhood. You can't fight with people and escape their neighborhood.

Almost everyone in the world has a personal story of pain, injustice, romantic upsets, and emotional hits that they've taken over the years as well as the rip-offs and the abuse they might have suffered, and all the times when they got their feelings hurt by others. Same as you. It's your special story, and you may feel justified and you may well have been an innocent victim, but you have to wonder in the overall karma of eternity if there really are any innocent victims.

If you believe in reincarnation, it might explain why there seems to be so much injustice and why you got hurt. Some people feel they're innocent, but if you know the underlying feelings and emotions, you can see how often they wound others in order to hurt them. Or they set themselves up through greed. They would often taunt others to create a confrontation. But if you knew the underlying feelings and emotions, you can see how they often taunt others to create a confrontation. Or they set themselves up through greed to suffer a loss.

But whether you are innocent or guilty or even partly guilty, or if you brought misfortune on yourself in some obscure way that you don't really understand, all that has to eventually become irrelevant for you now to proceed, because if you can't make peace with the world, you're stuck.

The injustice you feel is part of ancient stored pain, and that is inside of you. Some of it exists because of the sins of the father, or the mother, pain inherited down through the centuries, unresolved clusters trickling down through history. You will never escape the global karma or yours if you're perpetually locked into the energy of your ex-husband or your ex-wife or people that you've met on this journey through life. Let them go. You have to love your tormentors and offer them every warmth and goodwill that you can manage.

The hellish world is cold and seeks retribution and vengeance, while heaven is warm and embracing and forgiving. An eye for an eye, or a tooth for tooth, is a menu card for the reptile's banquet. It has no spiritual validity at all. Beyond the people you know that you pull to you in this life, you must also release and forgive and forget the karma of your social or tribal cluster. A cluster is a grouping of people, like a native tribe or even the members of the same golf club. It's pockets in the consciousness of humanity that are reflected in the mirror world, where similar mindsets and traditions gather together.

So the next liberation is the greater liberation of ditching what you were born with, the cluster.

For example, if you were born an African American, you most likely have the injustice of slavery as part of your life story. It'll be in your genes, in your subconscious memory, in the archetypes of your tribal mind, and because of this, you may see the white man as a villain and a tormentor, and you might feel threatened by him. So he sits inside your shadow self, and you are the victim. He is the slave trader.

But wait a minute. Do any African American slaves live in your hometown? Were you born a slave? Did you ever meet an African American slave? Unless you are about 150 years old, you're bound to answer no. So the terrible injustice of slavery is not really a part of your life. It's just a rotten story. The problem is, in having white men in your shadow as the enemy, you push away all the white men and women who might help you in this life, or give you a hand up.

Do you see how the tribal shadow is so destructive and holds you back spiritually? It's just the same for the Jews. They have their sad stories, and the Palestinians' story says how dark and nasty the Jews are, and so the Jews are inside the Palestinian shadow, as the Germans are inside the Jewish shadow, and so forth.

But all that terribleness is in the past. You've got to let it go. You have to guard yourself in the second liberation, the one that allows you to go beyond your religious, social, tribal, or national karma. You don't need it anymore, and you have to arrive to where you see yourself just as an eternal being, a loving, evolving spiritual being, not an African or a Jew, or a poor downtrodden Catholic in South America, or a disenfranchised woman. It's all story, nothing more, just a story.

Some of the story isn't even true, but it serves a purpose for unsophisticated people who have not resolved their shadow. They need this special story, and they need the memory of pain that was suffered in the past so they can feel squeaky clean now and holy. So they can garner money and compensation, for example, or sympathy—where they can feel they can get some special advantage as a victim, or they can get some special status.

Everyone in the cluster is allowed to feel angry all of the time. It's deadly. Because in order to step into another world spiritually, you have to more or less finish with the emotion of this one. I don't mean that you have to die, but you have to resolve the pain, understand it, finish it, stop complaining, and go past it. If not, you die spiritually weak, floundering. You die in the cluster of the wounds of your tribe, and you will drift to that part of the mirror world where wounded Jews are fighting with wounded Muslims or in a cluster of four million wounded Irish souls, people who died in the famine, and they all have the English in their shadow.

You can see how our human evolution is knotted and interlaced of my pain, your pain, and the collective pain.

If you can't go beyond the pain, you're stuffed; you'll float down the pain drain. Where does it lead? I know it's hard to go past the sense of injustice and the rage that certain political and social issues evoke, but we didn't incarnate into a world that is fair. We didn't come to a planet where people are respectful and caring of nature, the animals, and the environment.

The only option is to believe that there is a higher order of beings that watches over and protects, and they will not allow the planet to fall into absolute degradation and destruction. That is the third liberation, to see that it's our karma, and the planet's karma. It is to face injustice and to hold steady knowing there must be a resolution in the end, even if we haven't much evidence of it so far. It all exists at a higher level, because we exist at a higher level.

I think, in the end, all injustice will be set right and all sadness will melt away. Maybe not in our lifetime, but then, again, we might be in for a wonderful surprise.

A group of beings from another world has recently fought their way into this dimension, and we are waiting to see how that will affect things. All is not lost.

To summarize, the first liberation is to allow all those who have hurt you to go on their way, and in the second liberation, you let go of any clusters that trap you. In the final liberation you go beyond the anger and the pain of the terrible injustice suffered by the planet as an organism, and the animals and the general injustice people suffer every day.

If you're a sensitive person, the pain of the world will bother you, and we don't know why there has to be so much pain. It has a lot to do with the evil in our collective human shadow, but all you can do is process yours. You can't let yourself be overwhelmed by the global situation.

Your Journey through the Hidden Door

The hidden door beyond enlightenment I speak of is not a mythological place, nor do I speak of it in allegorical terms. It's real, it exists to be found, and I found it, and so have many others.

Just in case, you think I'm kidding, I have photos of human dematerialization. One was taken at my house in Australia. These are photos of people literally disappearing from this dimension. They're in a sensation, and we call it "morph."

In the next chapter, once I've laid out these introductory ideas, I'll talk a lot more about the world of the morph and how you can access it. It's hard to get a photo of dematerializations, as you can't set it up in bright light, you have to kind of flip the photo at the exact right minute, but my photos are real, and they are part of where this incredible journey has gotten to so far. When I discuss the gap and what lies in there for you to see and experience, just keep an open mind, if you will, and trust me without ever giving up any of your own reality.

I hope this book will help you not just to see the spiritual being that you are, but also to understand that there's a way of making peace with humanity, even inside what are often very restrictive, controlling systems that have enormous power over you. You can quietly wander off in your mind and your soul and eventually belong to something else.

This is not a hypothetical idea or airy-fairy promise, it's real. There's a gap in reality that is well known. You can walk through the gap to another world. I've taken hundreds of people, maybe a thousand there. Trust me, they've all come back safely. They didn't come back the same, but I didn't promise them they would be the same. I've promised them they would be different and more free.

I'm not here as another guru trying to convert the masses. What I have to offer is really for just a few people who are ready to walk away. For people who are really ready to go beyond transcendence and enlightenment and realize that they don't need it.

There's no dogma in the journey beyond enlightenment. I have a system here and it works, and if you want
to come with me, and if you've got the courage, I can
show you how you can find it yourself, your inner self,
your mirror self, your super knowing or higher self or
whatever you want to call it.

A Gentle Journey through the Three Liberations: A Guided Meditation

The following guided prayer and meditation is often
accompanied by the sound of a crystal bowl that
plays in the note of C. It's a gentle journey through the
three liberations and into a beautiful garden, where
you visualize yourself going through the hidden door
that I've been speaking about. Beyond that door, I
leave you on your own to experience the sound of this
celestial bowl. After about half an hour, come gently
back to the real world, to the normal state of consciousness. You might want to read the guided words
and play the recording to yourself. If you can find and
play the sound of the crystal bowl during this meditation (available on YouTube), your experience will be
enhanced.

Let's begin:

Find a comfortable place to lie down. Place your
head to the north and your feet to the south. Make sure

that your clothes aren't too tight, or that you won't be disturbed by outside noises or people coming in. Now as you begin to lie there and relax, take a slow and gentle breath. Hold it for a moment then exhale. Now take another slow, gentle breath. Hold it for a moment and exhale. Now take a third, slow and gentle breath. Hold it, hold it, hold it, and exhale.

Visualize yourself hovering ever so slightly above your body, only about six inches or so, and mentally, if you can, turn your head to where your feet are, and your feet to where your head is. Don't force it, and if you can't manage that visualization as yet, then leave yourself in the position that you find yourself. Take another slow, gentle breath. Hold it, hold it, and exhale going deeper and deeper, deeper and deeper.

Now I'd like you to visualize your feet going down through the floor, down through the bed that you're on, so that they are at 90-degree right angles to your physical body. Just hover there completely relaxed down through the floor, and in a second, I'm going to ask you to let go—to literally let go of the physical plane and allow yourself to fall downward in a straight line. Get ready. Let go. Now.

Feel the wind passing through your hair as you fall down and down, faster and faster. Imagine your hands by your side and allow yourself to go down feet first, and as you're going down gracefully through this place that you can't see, imagine that you've twisted just one turn to the right, and you continue to fall ever further, ever faster, straight down.

Gradually notice that you've come to the bottom and there you find yourself in a beautiful garden. Take a moment to look around this place. See how it impacts your feelings. Notice the colors and the softness. Notice its beauty.

Listen. See if you can hear small birds in the garden, the rustle of animals and insects. As you look all around, you notice this celestial place. Over in the distance there is a wall. Start to walk toward that wall. As you get closer to it, notice that there is a door inside that wall—the door to another world.

As you approach that door, notice there's an invisible force pushing against you, stopping you from proceeding. That invisible force is the three liberations. Find a comfortable spot in that garden, surrounded by all this eternity and all this beauty, and sit.

We will go through the Prayer of the Three Liberations because you will not be able to take them with you through the door.

When you find a comfortable place, bring up in your mind's eye, one by one, the people who have tormented you in this lifetime. Those who have caused you real pain. As you bring up each person in your mind's eye, breathe them in, and then breathe out toward them. Send them love and let them go. Tell them, *You are forgiven. I bless you. I release you. You may go now.* Go through each and everybody, and I'll leave you in silence for a few minutes.

As you complete the liberation of those people who have tormented you in this lifetime, your next thing is to go through and liberate yourself from the cluster of your tribal or social consciousness. Take a moment now to look at how that might have affected your life, how that inflicted certain rules and regulations upon you, and notice the heroic nature of those people and what they had to teach you.

Then gradually and slowly bring that whole cluster of your tribe or your social pattern up in your mind's eye, and, again, let it go. Tell it, *Thank you. I've learned through all of these things that you had to teach me.* Release that.

I'll leave you now for a couple of minutes while you think through the tribal clusters that you've come from and how you will now let them be.

As you complete going through the clusters, you understand that you have passed them now. The next liberation deals with justice and injustice. For some reason that we don't know, we incarnated upon this Earth plane, and the Earth plane is not entirely just. We're not alone. The animal kingdoms and the environment, they suffer as we do.

Take a moment now to look at the injustices that you've suffered in this lifetime, those things that form a part of your story, and as you bring them up in your mind's eye, lovingly release them. Realize that you don't need your story anymore.

Take a slow, gentle breath. Hold it for a moment, and exhale. Take another slow, gentle breath and hold it for a moment and exhale. Take a third slow, gentle breath, hold it, hold it, hold it. Exhale going deeper and deeper, deeper and deeper.

As you liberate yourself from justice and injustice, go on now to the animal kingdoms and the vegetable kingdoms and seek their forgiveness. Seek forgiveness for whatever injustice you have inflicted upon them.

As you look at that relationship for a minute or two, realize that they understand, just as you realize you have to understand and forgive the injustices that were perpetuated upon you. I'll leave you for a moment now in silence as you look at that and allow it to fall away.

Now as you complete the three liberations, I want you to rise up from your place in the garden and look around. You'll be surprised to notice that there is no wall, just a far country beyond the garden. I want you to turn to your left and now walk toward that far country and walk toward the bliss and the eternity that is part of the authentic you.

Let's observe silence now but only the sound of the crystal bowl for the next twenty-four minutes as you travel through those worlds watching and noticing what is there for you to know and understand.

When it is time for you to come back, back to the real world, I want you to turn behind yourself and notice that the garden is there once more in the distance. As you approach the beauty of that garden, I want you to once more enter into the feeling, the sensuality, the scent, and the flowers and the colors, and the little animals that might be about that area, the shade of the trees, the sound of running water. I want you to enter into that softness, the softness of the feminine spirit. Take a moment once more to observe the beauty of that garden.

Now as you make that garden a part of your inner self, a part of the authentic you, I want you to notice once more that the wall surrounds the garden again, because that is always how it is. It only opens for a short while, and then it closes.

Now it's time for you to return to the real world. I just want you to push up from the ground and notice that you can rise effortlessly. Look for a moment down-ward and notice that the garden is below you and start traveling up and up. Back to where your physical body is lying on the bed or on the ground.

Return now, reaching up, back for the physical plane. As you enter into the physical body, make sure that your head and your feet are aligned properly and that you're no longer hovering above your body. Just come back down into your physical body and remain still for the next few minutes while the memories of your journey play in your mind.

When you're ready, just rise up carefully and return to this experience, this incredible experience of being a human here on this planet at this time.

2

The Morph and
the Mirror World

In March 2001, I was at my house in Australia with about fifteen people. Suddenly, something very strange happened.

We were sitting in the front room where there were a number of daybeds, like those very large wide couches and sofas you see in movies in large Indian houses. Unexpectedly, on the face of one of the women there appeared a very beautiful geometric pattern. It was circles, dots, and triangles of many vibrant colors. The mysterious patterns oscillated, moved, and shimmered, and then they spread down her neck to cover her shoulders.

It was really awesome and mysterious to watch. There were no light effects in the rooms or sunlight from outside that could have caused it, and the patterns were not static like a shadow might be. They shimmered and changed positions all the time. It was quite a hot afternoon and one of the men had his T-shirt off, and he soon realized that he had the same patterns forming on his back.

Gradually, over a period of fifteen minutes or so, everyone had the geometric images come over their bodies, and every pattern was different. Some had blue stars and others had little red hearts, and some even had leopard skin patterns. There were all manner of possible fractal images and geometrics—as clear as anything to see.

This was the first time we ever experienced what became known later as the morph. It's a transdimensional phenomenon, an overlay whereby a room changes its imprint or ambience in the construct of space and time, and the surrounding reality takes on a new form. It is as if the room exists in two states at the same time, normal and solid looking, and abnormal and not solid at the same time. The walls go soapy looking, and the floor seems to become misty and disappears at times— even though you know you are standing on it.

Hazy striations began to swirl in the air and they floated together to form vortices and circles that you imagine you can travel down. They seemed to lead to another world. What we found to our amazement was that even our bodies seemed to go from solid to not solid. I know this might sound unbelievable, but myself and others have since seen the morph many thousands of times since that first time in March 2001. So the experience wasn't a one-off event.

I want to add here that we weren't on anything dodgy like hallucinogenics or drugs of any kind, just in case you are wondering. Everybody was stone cold sober and straight on that fateful afternoon that the morph first happened.

It's a new world, a supernatural one, descending on our 3-D world. It's the ultimate transcendental experience. For me, it's the most exciting thing that ever happened. It has completely changed our view of spirituality and extrasensory perception. The morph is for you and me and everyone.

What we found on that day when the patterns appeared was that our heads and our faces became less and less solid looking. We could see the bone structure and shape of a person's head, and then their face started to go hazy, and part of it would disappear completely. It would morph into another dimension. At times, we found that we could see right through each other, part of each of us was disappearing.

It wasn't scary. It was just intriguing. We found that the morph was everywhere all of the time.

When the morph is very strong, you can easily see it even in bright daylight, but usually it's much easier to see in a darkened room. It often looks like dry rain. If you want to see it, you have to learn to relax, and you have to learn to meditate if you don't already do so. All the dimensions and experiences beyond this world take the low brain wave pattern of the meditation state to get there.

Seeing the morph is nothing more than knowing and trusting it is there and deciding you want to see it, and knowing you see it if you care to. Try it when you are a little bit tired at the end of the working day, because that is when your brain cells oscillate at slower speeds. It's in the lower wave band of theta, which is 4 to 7 cycles per second, that the morph becomes clearer to see.

Action Step: Sit in a darkened room, or you can lie on a bed if you like, and focus on the idea that you would like to see the morph, knowing it is everywhere. The morph is around you right now. Try this process at night. Have the room almost dark with the lights off, but make sure there is just enough light through a crack in the door for you to be able to make out your hand when it is outstretched two or three feet in front of your face.

Now stare up at where the walls of the room meet the ceiling, and then bring your concentration back toward you. You are staring up at an angle of 45 degrees at the halfway place in the air of the room that is between the ceiling and your eyes, and suddenly you will see the morph there hovering. It is full of swirls and sparkling lights that look very much like small glowworms. We call the twinkling lights the *speckled ambience*. Its beauty evokes a sense of bliss and calls to some deep spiritual part of you. It's the grace of eternity that we all belong to.

Also in the morph you will see fast-moving diagonal lines crossing the room. That's the dry rain. Sometimes you might see a flash of light crossing your vision like silent lightning. Once you see the morph for the first time, you will see it all the time. You will also realize why you are further ahead than you believe yourself to be. You may have known for a while now that something is going on with the metaphysical reality of this world and you, but maybe you haven't had the right information to explain it. Sometimes the morph will be stronger than at other times, but it never leaves, so many of you have already experienced the morph without ever realizing it. The morph is here to change and heal the soul of the world.

Are you wondering why you would bother with all of this morphing? What reference or what relevance does it have on your spiritual journey? The morph, I tell you, represents the arrival of the feminine. Our world is a yang world. It's a world of outputs and a world of men.

It's a world of war and power and politics and acquisitions and materialism. The feminine spirit is the arrival of softness, compassion, healing, transcendence, ESP, and extraordinary happenings, like the ones I described before, where people dematerialized in a sitting room at my home.

With the morph, we're looking at the arrival of the opposite force. You might think this doesn't interest you, but in a way it's bound to interest you because it's going to intrude in your life, whether you like it or not. For example, this morph business has been around since the beginning of time because there are instances in the Bible where Jesus just appeared in front of his disciples mysteriously by sort of materializing in front of them.

Pals of mine have spontaneously levitated when they were lying on the bed, and suddenly they came up. Interestingly, they come up headfirst at an angle with their head high and their feet low, and eventually their feet were the last things to leave the bed. They'd be up there for several minutes and then come back down again. It's a mystery. I've never done levitation, so I can't say I'm an expert on it, but I know two people who have levitated three times between them. These are phenomena that we've learned from Hindu and Buddhist manuscripts.

The Yin Completes the Yang

These transdimensional worlds have been here since the beginning of time, but in our cerebral logical, very yang world, we lost touch with the hidden mystery that is all around us. We've lost it. Of course, we all know that in quantum physics, we are, for the most part, empty space; the nucleus of the atom is the only part that has any sort of reality to it.

The nucleus is minute. I mean, your entire body of nuclei wouldn't fit into a thimble. If we could collect all the nuclei and put them in there, you know, you're a dot on this page. So the idea that you're solid is only really our opinion because we need to be important. We like to feel we're solid, but we're not actually even solid. Which is sort of interesting because if you think you're suffering from a liver complaint, you're suffering from a liver complaint of a liver that isn't actually there, which is sort of weird. It's a thought form. It's ephemeral, the liver. Then perhaps you can just talk to this liver and ask it what it wants. It might say, *Well, I don't want so much whiskey. That's not helping me much, but I would like carrot juice or something.*

We can be so much more in touch with our humanity and with our physical body. As the feminine energy comes into this Earth plane, you have to imagine it as if you were lacing the fingers of your right hand through the fingers of your left hand. She (the yin) comes in, in the spaces between our reality, she's in the gap between our fingers. She completes us. We can't be complete in only a yang state. Even if you're in a woman, you live in a yang world, and you probably have to hurtle out to work every day, in a yang fashion and feed onto the freeway in the right place and feed off in the right place. You have to perform and be, so you may be feminine in your sexuality in your body, but you're living in and under the domain of male rules. The feminine spirit is moving in between the male, she's in between the molecules of our masculinity.

In ancient times many thousands of years ago, a group of beings appeared mysteriously in northern Italy, and they became known eventually as the Etruscan empire. They were centered around a small town in what is now Tuscany called Volterra. They had temples, and in those temples, the healers would lie down next to the person who was sick, and the healer would dematerialize and go inside the sick person, perform an operation, and come back out again.

Here we're looking at the spaces between the masculine and she arrives, the feminine, and she comes in. We have the potential to heal each other; we have the potential of being able to place our hand inside somebody and take out cells that might be cancerous. In the same way as Neo in the *Matrix* film puts his hand inside Trinity and takes out the bullet when she was shot. In that state in the *Matrix* film, he goes holographic, and she goes holographic.

In order to make that entry inside another person, you have to get into a holographic state. I've only ever had it happen to me once. We think we're separate, but, in fact, we're all one. There's only one person on this whole earth. Well, there are two, in fact—of the two people on this earth, there's only one male in the whole universe, and there's only one female in the whole universe, and we're all part of that oneness.

How to View the Morph

The sight of the morph is not something reserved for high adepts or Hindu holy men, or great spiritual leaders, the purple pooh-bah of the Seventh Ray, and all that malarkey. The morph is for everyone, and thousands of people have already seen the morph, and some like you will learn to use it. I'll show you how to get started.

Nothing like this has ever happened before in the history of psychic powers and metaphysical happenings. It's new, and lots of mystics and holy people and the Hopi Indians have predicted a New Age of enlightenment, and they were not wrong. It arrived. This truly is a new era for humanity.

I explained one way to see the morph earlier in this chapter. Another way to see the morph is to raise your arm in the air and watch the ends of your fingers— again in a darkened room—and see if you can see flashes of energy coming off the ends of your fingertips. The morph takes oxygen out of the air so it never comes down lower than two to three feet from your face. If you cup your hand and make a C shape with your forefinger and your thumb, try and see if you can see a small tube between the bottom of your finger and the top of your thumb. That little tube is a vortex.

Try putting a finger in the middle of the C that your forefinger and thumb make and as you push to the middle of that C you will feel it tickling slightly or it may feel slightly warm as it passes through another vortex. This morph thing is alive, and it also rejuvenates you.

One day my hand started to prickle like crazy, and I watched over a period of twenty minutes when all my cells rejuvenated and brown spots and pimples and faint blotches on my hand disappeared and the skin became creamy looking as if my hand had gone back thirty years in time. The gift of the morph will become a great power in this world, for when it showed me the rejuvenation of my left hand, it didn't happen on my right hand. Once the process was over, I could clearly see the difference between the two. In case you're wondering, the morph might have begun the healing process on you already.

Many of you have experienced the morph without ever realizing it. With the morph comes various body sensations—the most common begins with a twitching of the eye. This can last a few days or even weeks. At first, it worried me. I wondered what was wrong when this happened to me. I didn't know it was a morph thing, and then one day it ended.

Then there is what we call the *buzz*. It's a low-volume, high-pitched buzzing sensation that seems to move around your head. Often you imagine it behind you, as if it is hovering there, three or four inches behind the back of your skull. At about the base of your cranium, you'll sometimes hear the buzz move from one side of your head to another. Just like when you flip the speaker direction on a stereo system, and you hear that whoosh of the music going from side to side.

The buzz can be quiet and soft and gentle, and then other times it gets loud. Don't worry, it ebbs and flows, you'll get used to it. If you have the buzz, it's a gift, a grace that will develop over time. It's energy information coming from another world. The shamans of South America called the buzz the *airplane*; it seems to be part of the transdimensional journey and information download.

You may be familiar with a type of ringing in your ears called tinnitus. That is very different from the buzz because tinnitus is a medical condition in which the ringing is very clearly heard in one or both of your ears. The buzz, on the other hand, is more spatially located and moves around all the time. I've had it on and off for four years. Sometimes it stops for weeks at a time, and then it starts up again. At times, the buzz is less electric and loud, and it goes to a soft shushing sound, white noise, and is usually accompanied by a sense of bliss.

Then there is another audio sensation that you may have already heard, and that is what I call *formatting*. It's a very faint tick-tick sound, which seems to be limited to one ear. It reminds me of the sound floppy disks made in the early computer days, when you had to format them before use. I don't know as yet what the formatting sound represents, again, it feels like more downloads, but I do know what it looks like. Sometimes you will also hear the soft clicking of drumsticks. This is usually due to anomalies or fluctuations in the electromagnetic field around you.

These sounds are heard a lot in poltergeist investigations, which may not be the actions of evil spirits, but the warping of reality in places where strong electromagnetic fields cross, like in a valley where there are microwave phone towers on the surrounding hills. You may also have experienced what we call the *flutter*—the sensation that your nervous system is fluttering slightly. In men, it often starts between the legs, between the ankles, and women seem to first experience the flutter in the chest area.

I remember telling a doctor about the flutter, and he looked at me completely blank. He had no idea what I was talking about, and I've known people who scared themselves by thinking they had Parkinson's disease. However, the flutter is not an ailment. It is similar to the prickling that I felt on the back of my hand. It's a wonderful gift. If you get the flutter, it is marvelous. It's a high oscillation of life force or etheric as we call it, in which your cells begin to rebuild themselves by taking on a higher vibrancy.

Also, we noticed that people that have had the flutter over a period of years all look very bright and lucent, and often they begin to look younger and younger as time goes by. There are about 100 sensations of the morph, so I can't deal with all of them here, but some include a neck flip that occurs at night as you go to sleep, and a series of electric shocks in various places in your body, whereby your muscles twitch. Sometimes they're so strong, they can almost throw you off the bed. These *elecs*, as I call them, are big inputs of energy coming from another world. The morph to me is full of grace and beauty, and yet some of it is slightly weird because it's a world that we know very little about.

If at first you don't see the morph right away, don't worry. It could be because of two reasons. Some people are very cerebral. They are the world's thinkers. They have never been used to a world of subtle feelings, and they don't believe in the unseen. Often these people don't have visions or dreams whatsoever. They live just in a world of intellectual ideas. For them, everything has to follow logic, or they feel exposed and unsafe and open to ridicule.

If you're like that, give yourself time. You need to trust and let go, as your mind may be very bright, but it will never get to a place beyond enlightenment, for the transdimensional world we have discovered doesn't follow any logic that we understand.

There's nothing wrong with intellect and mind and logic, but it eventually runs out of answers. There are only ever questions and more questions. Sometimes people who are bright and intelligent, like university professors, have such powerful minds, they gradually make their minds into God; thinking becomes a religion for them. If you're like that, your life will be frustrating and hard.

But the only way humans can evolve beyond the mind is to enter into the supernatural. That world is not logical. It's fleeting, and perception is subtle. Some people are so coarse and cynical in their energy that they have no perception or very little, and their life becomes fearful, because they have difficulty in seeing the future. They don't believe that there is a grace or flow of divine light coming into their life.

The second reason for not being able to see the morph is that a long time ago you may have forgotten how to look. When you were a child, you would look and you would see. You could see the gap, the spaces between things. So start to look for what is not there, look into the spaces between the leaves, look and see if you can hold time.

There's a sensation that we call *fat time*, when the experience of time goes long and wide. If you know that feeling, you will have seen the edge of the gap. Start to look in the space between reality, between the leaves of the trees and so forth, and start to listen to hear what people are saying when they're not talking. Listen to hear what is in their silent dialogue.

You might also need a bit more of the flow of the God force or grace in your life. Without that you will be a bit blind for a while. You will feel a bit flat and ill at ease. You may be looking for energy to sustain you from outside sources—food, drugs, alcohol, sex, pornography, predatory ways, even thieving, and shoplifting—anything that brings energy from outside like incessantly watching TV. We do that because we seek momentary excitement. If you're cerebral, then you have to pray that the powers that be give you at least one experience that you can believe in, that will blow away the walls of logic. You'll get it if you pray for it and if you aren't too arrogant in the way that you pretend to know it all.

As you begin to believe, even if you can't see well right now, you can gradually pool the hidden power into your life, so the supernatural becomes more normal. Learn to sit or lie in silence in a semi-dark room and trust.

Action Step: You should keep a dream journal where you write down any dreams you remember, or visions, or even sudden strange sensations. Sometimes you'll be walking along and something would trigger a big realization. Jot that down, and bit by bit, those observations will come to form a pattern. It's your higher knowing from an inner world talking to you.

The trick is to embark on a plan to raise your energy and make yourself more aware of the gap. If your energy goes up, you'll feel more secure and less scared and you'll perceive more. There's a mass of information in the morph waiting for you to connect with it, and it will talk to you. I promise you, and even if at first you can't see, then you might have to create a threshold experience for yourself.

Here's one way: Set aside a few days when you're off work to be on your own and in silence out in nature up in the mountains. You might need to pull away from the stress and worry of your life and the day-to-day circumstances—for that can warp your image of self and corrupt your perception of life. This is because when we live in our emotions and our thinking, we lose connection with spirit, and the sacred nature of who we really are and what this life is about, which is remembering who you are.

A simple example would be if you have allowed your life to become repetitive and boring. Soon your mind comes to believe that nothing unusual could ever happen, and that life is always flat and dull. What you believe is what you see, and it's also what you get. So that dullness and a lack of imagination eventually becomes all that you see.

Sometimes your relationships are loving, and they sustain you. Sometimes they're so scary and so toxic, you lose sight of who you are, you forget to attend to yourself, you become a slave to the ideals of another to what you think they want from you. By getting away, you rediscover yourself, and you get to turn within and see what light is in there and how to guard it better.

I take time out to be on my own quite regularly. Sometimes I go on the road for months at a time, on my own, just traveling about. Such travel is vital to me. Yes, it can be a lonely journey, but in the quietness, or when walking in nature, I see beyond the boundaries of my life, and I see things I never saw before.

I also fast quite regularly as a way of bringing my energy up quickly. Sometimes I go without food for just three days, and sometimes I fast from five to nine days. If you have low blood pressure problems and other health concerns like diabetes, you shouldn't fast without discussing it with your healthcare professional because a small percentage of people don't do well by fasting, yet many others can benefit from it greatly. Fasting opens a doorway inside you very quickly. Your energy becomes instantly more rarefied and your mind goes quiet, and you become softer, more spiritual, and more aware of other worlds and unseen beings.

A threshold experience like three days of fasting in silence on your own can carry you from coarse and asleep, to aware and awake. Then suddenly, you'll see the morph even though you were looking at it all the time without seeing it before. The morph is there, and the morph is a lens for you to see inside these other worlds.

What Is Missing?

You may ask yourself why you need to go beyond enlightenment. Maybe you wonder why you would bother to make this journey, and I suppose the resounding reason is that if you look inside your soul, you'll see that there's something missing. Morpheus in *The Matrix* describes it as a splinter in your mind. You always know that there's something that isn't working. There's some bit that you don't know that you haven't found. You may be wandering around looking for the key to everything without knowing what the key looks like or what it is that you're actually searching for.

The reason for this journey beyond enlightenment, then, is really to arrive at the complete you, the authentic you, the whole you. The reason to make the journey and the reason to go into the unknown does take a certain amount of bravery, but then the yearning, the nostalgia for eternity that I speak of, is this thing we yearn to behold. (When I say unknown to people, they tend to get a little worried that I'm going to be whizzing them off into some sort of totally chaotic place. That's not true.)

We live almost entirely in a yang world, where we have no experience of yin whatsoever, and then the little yin that we do experience when we're out fishing or in the forest—or just moments where we're playing with our children on the beach at sunset—that's the only yin we ever experienced. Without the feminine, we aren't complete, so the morph represents the arrival of the feminine and the journey beyond enlightenment, which, of course, is an ego trip enlightenment. It's a spiritual elitism, it doesn't exist, but the journey beyond enlightenment is saying, *Hey, what I want is completeness. What I want is wholeness. What I want is to arrive back to where we all came from.*

Some of you may ask, *Why am I on the journey and why am I not necessarily pushing you to go?* I'm just doing that out of my typically English politeness, because I don't want to scare you or challenge you or want you to feel inadequate, but, of course, you'll go on the journey, and the weird thing is you don't go on the journey, the journey comes to you.

It's the same way with bilocation. Bilocation is the ability to go into a trance or move your body a great distance in seconds, by sort of bending space-time. Attempt to travel from, let's say, Texas, to France, but in fact, the only way you can bilocate is if you can pull France to you. In other words, at the point where you make this trans-dimensional transition, Paris comes and gets you.

How you arrive beyond enlightenment is not to strive to arrive at it. Because in the striving, you engage these yang emotions, the intensity of your intention, the intensity of driving and pushing and wanting to arrive, the intensity of not feeling good enough. You may think if you take on these spiritual practices, you'll be better and more holy, but this journey has nothing to do with better and holy. Better and holy is completely irrelevant. You can't arrive at God other than in your imperfect state, because we are imperfect, and so in the striving, you'll never get there. It's almost as if the more you strive for the holy grail, the more the holy grail hops up the road in front of you.

That's why so many people are so desperate to have one spiritual experience (if only Jesus would appear on the refrigerator or If Mary would appear on this tortilla, they could sell it on eBay for twenty grand). In their desperation to achieve that holy grail, they just push the holy grail up the road in front of them. Because they're pushing, they are operating out of the yang, so the intensity of wanting it forces it to keep away from them, but when they're no longer forcing it, it comes to find them.

The trick is to not push. It's not so much retreat, because you don't want your feelings to be any less than before. You don't want to create a sense of defeat, and you don't want to create a sense of inactivity but more a gentle intention. You're wandering along, you're prompted to read this book, you're prompted to call a friend, you see something strange and you think, *Wow, I don't know why but I'm pulled to the Native American and I'm going to go to visit the Anasazi ruins.*

This whole world is so perfectly organized. There's no chance. There's no accident. Nothing is misinterpreted. Nothing goes wrong. It is all absolutely perfectly organized. That's sort of like the divine plan.

The way to make this journey is passively, and that's why women never experience anything like the amount of fear that the men experience because we men are not passive. We're way more controlling. It's the natural yang thing, to control and to organize and to stimulate, and we put boundaries on everything. We want to rule the world, and if we can't rule the world, we want to rule the town, and if we can't rule that, we want to rule the street, the neighborhood, or just our families. Women are much more passive, and the whole thing is this passiveness. So it isn't frightening unless you hold on. It isn't frightening unless you resist.

Yes, strange things will happen, but allow them; you just allow it to happen, and what you'll know from experience after a while, if you're a little bit of a spiritual warrior and have been on the path a bit, is that none of this stuff ever lasts more than fifteen or twenty minutes, and you'll get some really bizarre sensation that's gone in three days.

It's like if you come home and somebody's stolen your stereo system, you can go into a panic and a rage. Or you could just say, *Well, they've come for the system.* Everything you own, you've only borrowed from God. Like it's a big rental yard in the sky. You don't own everything you borrowed. You aren't taking any of it with you. You're just borrowing it for the space of this lifetime or a few years and it's the same with your stereo system. You can go mad because it's been stolen. Or you could acknowledge that somebody else has borrowed your system now.

In this book about the journey beyond enlightenment, I have offered you the potential of an extraordinary journey. You don't have to accept that potential. You can continue along this life that you've built for yourself, but it will be regimented. It will be tick-tock, ho-hum, boring. It will oppress you. Most people figure out a way to oppress themselves and/or kill themselves rather than change, and it's not for me ever to say that is wrong or that is right. I don't know what's right for you, but where you feel the splinter in your mind, where you feel the frustration, where you feel that inadequacy, then that will impel you to move forward.

I remember ten and fifteen years ago, I would lie in my bed at night, and I would cry, because I thought my life was so utterly futile. In those days, I had an ivory tower better than anybody else's—a thirty-room mansion and servants and cooks and gardeners. I had millions in the bank, and I was rocking around like a pop star, stretch limos and all, suites in the fancy hotels, and all that was fine. It was a wonderful experience.

But in the end, I gave it all away. I gave away the mansion. I spent most of the money going from one place to the next, and what was left of my money, I gave it away and eventually went with a suitcase of $50,000 that I kept for myself. I'm still on the journey. My ivory tower was my enlightenment in a way because, at the end, I realized I didn't want to keep it up, and circumstances sort of conspired to collapse my ivory tower anyway.

The Doorway to Spiritual Heaven Goes Sideways

Consider this psychological flip. You have to make people think that higher is up, but energy that is moving faster is not really going up. It's going sideways. If you ever meet a man or a woman who truly knows these worlds that I'm speaking about, you will notice that they've come off the roof of the tower, and they're going sideways, not up.

Now you can troll through the Bible and great works and all of the New Age literature, and you can benefit from the ideas of great teachers, but you'll never find people who will tell you that the etheric goes sideways. This is because they all think as the ego would—an ego that has lived on the ivory tower all of its life. The fool only understands up, but sideways is the right answer. It took thousands of years before we found that out.

Jesus might have ascended into heaven after the crucifixion. I can't say if that is true or not. Christians have to take it on faith, but I can tell you this: if Jesus ascended into heaven, he didn't go up, as there's no up to go to. If you go up, you get into altitude problems and your lungs collapse.

If he went anywhere, he went sideways. He ascended to heaven sideways, and maybe he dematerialized. That is because the doorway to the spiritual heaven we all seek in at 90 degrees to us, at right angles. Light travels in a straight line at about 300,000 kilometers per second, but what people don't usually realize is that light also has a sideways motion at 90 degrees to the straight line ahead that light is taking as it travels through space. There is a zigzag sideways motion to light as well as to the forward motion of light.

The zigzag motion of light is described in a special type of mathematics that is called the *mathematics of imaginary numbers*. If you wanted to dematerialize and enter into a heavenly dimension, you would have to learn to slide across sideways; you have to follow the transverse wave of light. You can trust me on that for two reasons. First, everyone who has ever tried to make it by going up failed miserably, and second, the sideways motion is the only way you can ever go backward in time, as that is the only way you can go faster than light.

It's not your physical body that will travel faster than light—but it is your third body, your life force, to evolve beyond the tick-tock world. You have to think out of the box and fall back on yourself in that sideways world. Let me explain.

The laws of light refer to the forward motion of light in a vacuum, but the sideways motion of light is not very fast at all. In fact, the waves of the sideways motion oscillated about 4000 to 8000 angstroms a second (each pulse wave is known as an *angstrom*). So you have to imagine 4000 to 8000 zigzag lines crossing the main light beam every second. If you can oscillate your life force, the etheric, sideways at over 8000 cycles a second, you will actually be going faster than light.

Nothing physical can move faster than light, but the human etheric can move sideways faster than light, and that has now been proven in the morph over and over. The sideways motion will grant your perception of the future, and you will need to know that because you have to be able to understand the karma of nations and people, and you will have to make critical decisions at exactly the right time.

You will have to be able to see the future. Don't worry, it's easy. When you lie down to meditate, or even if you meditate sitting in a chair, first imagine yourself sliding off to the right. It's a creative visualization. And even if at first you can't get your etheric to respond to that sideways order, you can make it happen over time by imagining it, and the etheric always follows your imagination.

You see how clever this system is? The tower is up with more and more gratification, more illusion, and all the stress and futile depression, and the struggle to sustain self-importance, but once the tower comes down, and the ego is tamed, and sometimes humbled, you have nowhere to go but to travel sideways. This travel takes you toward a warrior existence with other people and toward the animals and toward Gaia and the healing of the planet, and all the natural domains of softness, love, compassion, and acceptance. Sideways takes you to where you eventually know that you haven't got a clue. In fact, the more you grow and become truly transdimensional, the more you will know for certain that you don't know very much at all—none of us do.

All I'm telling you here is how to get to the 90-degree nowhere land. I can't begin to describe the fractal worlds beyond the door where the higher beings exist from beyond the void, and as I said at the beginning of this book, at the very end of this journey, there's nothing, just the eternal void, and that void is nothing and everything.

Looking back from that void, enlightenment looks silly. It's just a term invented by spiritual elitists; you have to engage the ego and your mind to be enlightened. You don't need it. It's far too heavy. In the void, there is nothing in every direction. In the vastness of nothing, what point of reference would you use to decide whether you're up or down, enlightened or not enlightened?

Let me explain.

Pause and imagine yourself in the void, and that there is nothing, no family, no friends, and no sounds, no up, no down. No hope, blank, nothing. The way to visualize it is to imagine looking down and seeing an endless darkness and blackness below you. That will give you the right impression. Or you could ask in a meditation to show you the void, but you have to hang on to your hat if the beings come to handle your request.

After the void, I could see that humanity's insistence on the ivory tower looks silly. It's just childlike, not real, worthless, and all the little things of life look gracious and marvelous, and they're worth everything.

Make it a part of your energy plan to get rid of one aspect of the ivory tower every day if possible. Today, sell a second car; tomorrow, give away some of your designer clothes; and the next day liberate yourself or something or someone. Every day some part of the ivory tower goes, and then get rid of a bad habit and then lovingly settle an argument with someone and, the following day, sell some more of your accumulated rubbish and use that to settle a debt and so forth.

I did an inventory of the people in my life. You might want to do the same as part of your threshold plan. Write down the names of all the people that you know and deal with and their impact on your life. Family, friends, business associates. Then sit quietly and bring them up in your mind's eye. How many really love you and support you and accept you unconditionally? And how many are a waste of time? Or do they feed off you emotionally or drain you energy-wise or money-wise?

How many are honest and how many of them are dead dodgy? How many lie to you? I've always found if a person lies about small things, they will eventually lie about big things, and when you come upon a person who doesn't deal with absolute truth in their life, then whatever energy expressed in their direction will eventually bring tears and heartache.

Embracing the truth is a sideways move. Catch yourself every time you exaggerate or bend the truth, every time you deliberately give people an erroneous impression, or when you offer them faulty facts. Learn to become scrupulously honest, make a point of noticing when you're in denial and when you're glossing over events, interpreting them in a bent or dodgy way to suit your story. Try to be honest with yourself and agree to live like that, in an impeccable way as much as possible. Remember, of course, that none of us is perfect.

Understanding the Memory of Feelings

The reason for this effort is that over in the mirror world, the you that is in there, that is composed of your subconscious feelings and impulses, has to operate from the perspective of the authentic soul that you really are. So naturally that you cringes every time you go the other way, and you're dishonest or covert, and every time you act dishonestly with yourself, or you act outside what is proper and correct. It's trying to prompt you all the time in your dreams, and by firing through subtle feelings that prompt you to go toward what is healthy and truthful and beneficial, and away from phony and lies and darkness.

Those feelings are stored in the mirror self, which is your eternal spiritual identity. It's not so much about what happened in this life. It's more about how you felt about what did happen, and how your actions in this life affected the feelings of others. In other words, your whole life comes down to a memory of feelings. Some of you have always known it was about the feelings, and perhaps you were scared to say so—by feeling ridicule or feeling that you would seem to be slightly dippy or that you would be marginalized. But you were right all along, and the world around us and the one we see on TV is the world of yang and ego and thinking, war, power, money, glamour, fame, up, up, up; these things are seen to be so important and special.

Yet in a hyperspace reality, it all matters very little, if at all. It will all be swept away in the end, none of it lasts. Only the human feelings last, and they're stored in your subconscious, which is here and in the mirror self. The mirror self is, in effect, your soul. That is beautiful. That's where the perpetual long-term memory of you is kept.

I think I worked that out before I could actually see the mirror world. Here's how. Ages ago I began to wonder what mechanism or recording device actually remembers you after the brain ceases. Obviously, a lifetime of events and struggle here on Earth will be meaningless if there was no mechanism for remembering what actually happened to you. There couldn't be an afterlife without a mechanism for remembering, yet no religion or spiritual philosophy in the world has ever properly explained what holds or retains the perpetual memory of you after death.

But via the morph, we saw that we're all in the mirror world before we die in an alter ego in a mirror world identity. Then the remembering problem was suddenly solved.

Once your brain ceases functioning, the memory of you here is lost, but your mirror self in the spirit world opposite us has all the information anyway, and it continues to exist in its own dimension. It isn't dead. How cool is that? Problem solved. Your mirror self has your deep innermost feelings. It doesn't affect your soul.

In the morph, you can actually see it. Imagine the thrill of seeing your soul. It doesn't seem credible, but it's in there. The Bible talks about people losing their souls, but in the perpetual memory of the mirror world, I don't think you could lose your soul. It's eternal.

In 1930, Paul Dirac discovered a mirror world of antiparticles or antimatter that is opposite to the solid world. Dirac's mirror world doesn't look any different from our 3-D solid world, except the antiparticles are of an opposite charge. Your antiparticle self would look like your twin. It is thought that at the beginning of time, the negatively charged antiparticles destroyed the positively charged particles.

Therefore, what we see as our universe is the remnant of those explosions. Scientists speculate that there must have been a slight excess of positive particles over the negative antiparticles. The ratio is estimated to be one extra positive particle in every billion particles. So you're one in a million or one in thousands of millions actually.

When You Hate, You Hate Yourself

You should write down those things that are tormenting you. You have to learn to love your tormentors because they're you, and in placing blame on others, what you're really doing is blaming yourself. If you see inadequacy in that person, then it's your own inadequacy that you're projecting. If you feel that these people are being dishonest, it's because you've always been dishonest.

We hate people that we love. When you hate a person, what you really mean is there's something about them that you love. They have something you want. One of the steps of the journey beyond enlightenment is to begin to own what you're looking at, to begin to own your own emotions.

Again, as I said, it's all to do with a resonance of the imprint of your feelings, and so if you hate them, it's because you hate yourself. Or it's because they've got something you want, or because you're jealous of them, or because you feel that they're competing with you.

But as I've always said, when a person wants to compete with you, let them. Let them win, agree to be last. Go into the next race, the next game, the next whatever and agree to be last, and if you are ahead and you're close to the line, trip over, fall down, lose your shoe, get lost, but make sure you don't win. Even though it says in the great book, the last shall be first and the first shall be last, most people don't listen. They're up on the freeway at six in the morning and they're driving fast and trying to be first. *Hey, wait a minute, you don't want to be first; you want to be last. That's the safest place to be.*

In talking about this inner torment that we create for ourselves, a lot of people suffer from the need to be perfect, then that usually comes from a projection that they received in childhood, from their less-than-perfect mother and their less-than-perfect father. So if the father failed as a football player, he wants his son to become the world's greatest and he'll torment his son to make it to the Super Bowl.

We always get that need for perfection from our parents. Or we get it from the people that you go to school with. So you feel you have to be perfect to compete with them. Don't compete with them. That's the same thing as agreeing to be last by agreeing to lose. You don't need to be perfect. We didn't come to be perfect. It's just a torment that you inflict upon yourself. It's a psychological tormentor for no reason at all.

One day I was in Florida, and I decided to walk through the ghetto. It was two o'clock in the morning. I took off my shoes because being like a white man walking through the ghetto at two in the morning is a slightly dangerous experience for an English tourist. So I took my shoes off actually to disarm anybody who might wonder why this man was walking along carrying his shoes.

I met a very nice man called Slim who took me through the ghetto, and I was there for two hours wandering around the streets. I went to a bar with him, but about four o'clock in the morning, I wound up on the sidewalk, outside the ghetto, like a block outside, and I didn't have any money on me because I'd given all my money away when I was in there. I had had maybe $200 or $300 in my pocket, and when I came out, I realized I didn't have a dime. I didn't even know the address of my friend's house where I was staying because he had driven me there. I just knew what street it was off.

Four policemen showed up and they were standing over me asking me questions: *Who are you? Why are you here? Why are you sitting on the ground? Why don't you have your shoes on?* They were really aggressive, so I stood up and I said to these police officers very quietly but very softly, "My name is Stuart Wilde. I'm an English tourist. I've been wandering around the district here tonight, visiting people."

I said, "I demand that you love me and protect me," and they all went really quiet. These massive police officers that looked like the front row of the football team, all dressed in black with their guns (we're not used to guns from England) just looked at me.

I said, "I demand that you protect me and love me."

Suddenly they just softened right up. Finally, one asked, "What do you need?"

And I said, "Look, I'm really stuffed. Because I don't know where I am, and I went into this neighborhood, and I gave all my money away to various people who asked me for it. What I really need is a quarter so I can call my friend [from a pay phone] and ask him to come and collect me."

So the officer gave me a quarter, I made a phone call, and my mate showed up. For the fifteen minutes we waited, the policemen stood over me. They wouldn't leave me there because they said I was going to get killed. It was four in the morning, and I said, "I don't think so, sir, because I've already been wandering around for a couple of hours. I didn't get killed two hours ago. Why would I get killed now?"

But they insisted. So these four guys, like the Four Horsemen of the Apocalypse, were standing over me until my mate showed up to pick me up.

When you're less than perfect, and you stuffed it up and you break the vase, you say, *Look, I'm sorry, I broke the vase, love me. Just love me. I'm sorry. I'm late, love me. Sorry, I was really grumpy, love me. Sorry, I didn't meet the deadline. I'll try harder next time. Love me. I'm sorry, I wrecked your car, love me.*

You've got to be careful not to use this *love me* routine as a way of being totally inadequate all of the time, or fobbing people off. Because the whole secret in life is you have to become a custodian and not only with your own feelings, but with other people's feelings. You have to put yourself in their shoes and understand how they feel about the fact you've wrecked their car.

You have to care for their feelings, but in many ways, if you go through the world demanding everybody loves you, they will, you know, *I want you to love me.* You know if they're angry with you, say, *Look, I really understand that you're angry and I'm sorry, I've let you down but love me.* It automatically sets up that you do love in return. *Love me.*

I'm not perfect. I don't know for myself either. I don't have a perfection to offer. I have no wizardry. I make softness in my own heart my wizardry. You know, I have no plan. I'm like walking gently every day. I don't have a plan. That's my plan. They ask, *Why don't you have a plan?* You see, because plan is yang. It's intellectual. It's expecting the same things to happen next week that happened this week. How many millions have been lost on the stock exchange on that kind of plan?

When you get to a crossroads, you don't know which way to go. You can struggle and you can tear and beat at your chest and pull on your blouse or whatever, trying to work out which way to go. Excuse me, if you arrive at a crossroads and you don't know where to go, there's only one answer: go nowhere. Stop and pitch your tent. That's it. Stop right there. Don't go anywhere. Because if it's not in your feelings, if it's not coming through from the mirror; if it's not coming through from your soul, then why would you go anywhere?

It's All Real in the Geometry of Your Destiny

I'm almost certain that you will see the morph because it's everywhere, and let this book act as a doorway for you. There's a mechanism of alignment available to you. It's just in the knowing. There's a sort of amnesia that goes on, and, of course, in childhood, we see all sorts of beings and all sorts of magical things that later in life as grownups we'd completely glossed past.

I remember visiting with a truly legendary ayahuasca shaman from South America. I was saying to him, "Are these beings real, and are these experiences real?"

He said, "It's all real. It's just you pretend that it isn't real."

So you will have lain in your bed and you would have seen beings walking through your room, because it was ephemeral, and it was at the side of your vision, and you just glimpsed them. You made nothing of it or of strange coincidences. You kind of brushed them off, but there aren't any coincidences. That's all part of the geometry of your destiny, your life.

I should reiterate here that it's in the silence, that's in the softness that you learn. That's how you get to this femininity. That's how the right hand laces the left hand, the yin moves in between the spaces of yang. I've read a lot of books, I've studied a lot of stuff, and I'm knowledgeable of metaphysical spiritual writings. But almost everything I've ever learned has been learned in the morph. The morph is very feminine; the morph is water and looks like water.

It's the presence of the feminine spirit that has descended upon our planet, in the silence, in the softness. If you have a lot of obligations, you might say, *I don't have a lot of time for silence.* I understand that, but in a few moments of silence you have just touched inside your heart. Breathe in and hold that breath, and imagine yourself spreading to the outside of the universe faster than the speed of light. You can embrace the entire humanity, planet, solar system, and the universe, and then breathe out and breathe in again.

If you only have ten minutes of silence, while you're waiting for the train to come to take you to work every day, use that ten minutes, not listening to your mind rambling on about the mortgage payments, but a soft moment where you connect with a God force within, where you remember the nostalgia that you have for eternity.

Eventually, you should be able to access those other worlds just by knowing how to do it. It's like a click of the mind where you see what others don't see. It doesn't take a rocket scientist, but it does take a certain amount of courage. For as I've said before, there are places deep inside you that you have yet to discover and unearth, and you have to allow that to come out and understand it.

But that is all part of the heroic compassion of self I spoke of, and an understanding that none of us is perfect. We're all white and some black. So as a spirit, you and I are mostly gray, neither a saint nor devil, some-place in between. We're all fallen angels doing our best. Get up, let's move on. We don't seek perfection. There's no such thing. We only seek to redeem ourselves, and hopefully, we will help others realize the same peace and redemption. This is what this is all about: deliverance, deliverance from evil, deliverance from dark influences, many of which you can't see now.

I'll talk about the inner and outer matrix in the next chapter, along with deliverance from the despair and confusion of a lack of understanding, back to the light, and an eternal happiness and peace. You look inside the morph in a meditative state and you lie still and wait and see what visions and information it offers you, and all you need is to try the exercises I suggested and raise your energy a bit if you have to, and you'll see it right away.

There's a mechanism at work here. So the very fact that you are reading this book was your destiny to do so, and so that means a chance will be offered to you. Not by me, of course, as I don't have the power of yes or no over humanity, but by the forces of light that operate the hidden door I spoke of. Some people see the mirror world easily as a continuous series of actions playing in their mind's eye like a video clip, and others don't see it right away, but they do see pictures bit by bit as visions and the story of that world and their reality in it starts to unfold, usually as fast as they can embrace the gap that I spoke of previously.

In the next chapter, I will explore more about the memory of things and the resonance that you leave behind you as you go along.

3

Explore the Inner Sound of Your Soul

Let's look at the resonance and the sound of your soul, its stately other-world imprint. In the last chapter, I introduced the idea about how the mirror world is opposite us, and in that there is an alternative view. It is composed of your inner most subtle feelings that come from your subconscious mind. We say it is the real you, the authentic you.

The alternative self is sacred. It holds the perpetual memory of you. That inner you has a resonance and that resonance is like a sound. So you could say your soul has a tone that typifies what it is, and that tone may be very ancient and mysterious. It may resonate at a level that is way beyond anything you've ever heard here on Earth.

For beyond the mirror world are other worlds. Each of us has spread through layers of eternity—like strips of chocolate through the center of a sponge cake—and the resonator of that celestial tone here on Earth is your heart. It throbs out the feelings that are remembered in your soul, and those are emitted initially from your heart chakra. It's a pulse or a signal, one that is U shaped. That pulse is very fast moving. It travels through the etheric waves that surround your body and out from there to others.

Those signals you give off imprint reality around you—just as Professor Emoto's water crystals are changed into beautiful snowflake shapes, or horrible ghoulish images, depending on the feeling of the word that is written on the glass tube that holds the water. If your heart is very big in the sense that you're an open and loving person, someone who has come to accept humanity unconditionally with no personal judgment—if you have proved that by serving people, and if you see life as a sacred gift, then it is possible that the tone of your soul could resonate for many miles, right across the city.

You would have the silent power to bend what has become ugly and dark back to beauty and symmetry. When the heart tone is very beautiful, it's very deep in its resonance. The closest here on Earth is the sound of a crystal bowl. Check YouTube videos, as I suggested earlier with the guided meditation, to hear this sound. Once you hear the crystal bowl, you can understand how the resonance carries you off to another place. It's a healing tone. If you listen carefully, you can feel yourself going down the center of the sound to another dimension. When you listen to the purity of a crystal bowl, you know it's a pure note of C. It has a pristine, uncluttered quality to it. So that is what our soul really is. It's that sound.

When the world ends, there's going to be one thing and one thing only, and that's the sound of water. When you listen to the sound of water, you're listening to the symphony of the end of the world, and inside that C note is this absolute pristine purity, this uncluttered purity, like when an opera singer hits a high C. That is the most inspirational part of the song.

If you have ever listened to, let's say, *Madama Butterfly*, when the opera singer hits that high C, it carries you back to God; your whole skin starts to tingle, and it doesn't matter if you're into heavy metal and rock or whatever, an opera singer who can hit that singular note carries you out of the way.

That is the nature of the eternal spirit within us. I'm not saying that heavy metal is evil, but it's like a clatter of the chaotic ego. It is the music of chaos. It's the music of disgruntled, pained people who are going to clash and bang and make as much noise as possible. Lots of people love heavy metal. It talks to them in some way that they appreciate like, with some, jazz is the music of despair. Jazz was invented by the Black Americans coming up from the fields. They sang about the pain or the torment of their life and sometimes they sang about beautiful things, but you can't listen to jazz unless you want to do a bit of despair. It's the music of despair.

Let's look at your etheric energy and see what can be done to make it prettier and more resonant, and by raising the vibration to oscillate faster, we hope to disengage from disease and discordant dark energy and align to a purer, more beautiful world. Let us discover what the song of your soul sounds like, but first, let me discuss the etheric fields and bio-photons.

Glimpse into the Etheric Field

Twenty years ago, I discovered I could see the etheric field around trees. It's the flashing oscillation of the life force around all living things. Then I saw it around humans and animals, and finally, when my senses got stronger, I realized it's around everything such as plants and bugs. The etheric is full of fast-moving vortices and striations of hazy light.

Later I came to see many more complicated ramifications in the fields. In many ways, author Carlos Castaneda was right when he said that we walk around in a luminous egg. The etheric stretches out several feet in all directions.

I learned that our human feelings are in that field. What we normally describe as feelings are just sensations, electrical pulses to the brain, and the emotions are our reactions to those pulses—pleasure, pain, happiness, anger, and so on—but real human feelings of love, hate, frustration, and joy are all in the etheric. That is how you can read people accurately and sometimes help them. You pick up on their hidden feelings they emit by touching their etheric with your mind, or by placing your hand on their chest, for example.

Here's a bit of a scientific background to the etheric reality. Researchers have discovered a new particle, a very weak one called a *bio-photon*, which is part of the light spectrum. It is measured with highly sensitive equipment. The bio-photon seems to be given off from all living things, and it is thought to be light emitted from the DNA. The discovery of the bio-photon seems to confirm the existence of the etheric field around our bodies as a scientific fact. A photon is a packet of light. So a bio-photon is a particle of light given off by a biological system, like the human body. The light given off from a glowworm would be another example of light from a biological source.

The bio-photon was discovered by medical scientists in Russia in 1923. They originally gave it the strange name of *mitogenetic rays*, but nothing much came of that theory until they were rediscovered by the German biophysicist Fritz-Albert Popp. He was the scientist who said the biological light came from the DNA, and that it had a coherent quality—meaning that it was like laser light. Laser light travels a long way because the particles of light are in a tight coherent field bunched closely together, so the light doesn't spread out and dissipate like the light beam of an ordinary flashlight.

The coherence is the same for the etheric light around your body. That is why you can fire your etheric using your concentration and the power of your will. You can send it across the street, and someone who can see the etheric even a little bit can watch you doing it.

Professor Popp has suggested that certain diseases may be due to a drop-off in resonance in the bio-photon field emitted by the body. It has also been suggested people are influenced by remote sources of etheric light, which has led to research into distant healing, and it may explain why certain magical healers can breathe on people or touch them and make them better. It's also why we seek to raise the energy of the etheric and make it go faster.

The researcher, William Hamilton III, has said and I quote, "This light emission is an expression of the functional state of the living organism, and its measurement therefore can be used to assess the state. Cancer cells and healthy cells can, for instance, be discriminated by typical differences in bio-photon emissions. In other words, sickness is darker than health."

After the initial decade and a half of basic research on this discovery, biophysicists of various European and Asian countries are now exploring the many interesting applications, which reign across such diverse fields as cancer research, noninvasive early medical diagnosis, food and water quality testing, chemical and electromagnetic contamination, cell communication, and various applications in biotechnology.

In theory, the bio-photons of the etheric field can't be seen by the naked eye, but in subdued light, the etheric is clearly visible, and thousands of people all over the world can see the etheric on a regular basis. I've never thought that the sight of it took any particular spiritual or psychic gift. All you have to do is learn to tilt your head slightly. When viewing things in subdued light, like a tree, say, at dusk, look at the top of a tree, and then move your attention a little way to the right and stare at the sky there, and without moving your eye, take your concentration back to the top of the tree and you'll see the life field. You'll see the etheric of the tree.

If you're interested in morphic resonance, in the fields of information around living things like the etheric, you might like to check out the work of biologist Rupert Sheldrake. Sheldrake said we are all surrounded by fields of information that he calls *morphogenic fields*, and those fields direct the way an organism develops. So a giraffe is giraffe-shaped because it is surrounded by a morphogenic field that has the history of all the giraffes that have ever lived on Earth.

Popp has also speculated the bio-photons are message carriers, and that they may be responsible for ESP and nonlocal jumps of information in quantum fields. *Nonlocal information* is when quantum particles jump, and they disappear in one place and appear in another place. For example, nonlocal information would be when you intuitively know that your friend is sick or in need of help, or just when you intuitively know that the phone rings and you know it's Aunt Maude before you even pick it up. You just got a hit that it's Maude.

You find that gradually, as you let go of the sort of ivory tower of analytical logic, you enter more into the sideways space of feelings, that you become connected to the global feeling, and there you can be fully aware how it feels in Palestine today, or fully aware of the problems that are happening in the ecology of the tundra, let's say. You become connected to the Gaia of the planet, and you're connected to people.

It's through this bio-photon etheric field that we develop ESP and intuition, and I have lived the whole of my life like that. I don't really make intellectual decisions. I tried to look around corners with my etheric intuition with my feelings. I'm more looking at how does the thing feel. I can look at a person and I can tell you parts of their life story, just from their feelings, not from how they look. They can be dressed in a bunny rabbit outfit, but just from the imprint that they make walking through a hotel lobby, I can tell you where that man is going with his life.

The Body's Intuition

This awareness is completely about gaining more energy for yourself because not only are you acutely aware of the humans that you are in service to, but you're acutely aware of what you need. Therefore, you'll get these strange little pieces of information that suddenly tell you to eat fennel. You think fennel. I never eat fennel. What is fennel? But there it is in the supermarket, and you just go and you eat fennel, because inside fennel there's some mysterious molecular structure that your body desperately needs. It's an intuition about your body. It's an intuition about business opportunities. It's an intuition about people, especially people that sort of look okay, but they're not. You can sense they're going to let you down or rip you off.

It's an empathy. I don't know really quite how to describe it, but it's like when you watch a bird. The bird is flying inside your soul, so when the bird tips its wings from one side to the other, you can feel that wing shift inside your heart. You can feel the spirit of a little dog. His heartbeat is inside your own heartbeat. I'm describing an empathy for humanity and an empathy for nature.

The ivory tower is created by electricity, and it's created by the ego and its incessant needs; it's sort of the opinion of the personality. Your personality has opinions and those opinions feed the ivory tower. The ivory tower is always a situation of separation. The idea for the ego is to separate itself from humanity. The ego wants to be higher than other people—even if it's only two or three other people—but it still wants to be higher, like the certain sort of homeless people who are sleeping in the park and want to be higher than the other homeless people. It's this idea of separation.

The ivory tower creates a personality that wants to be separated from humanity, and there's a reason in quantum physics for that—because in quantum physics, nothing exists until you observe it. So a particle is in a hyper-state, a potential of being somewhere, but it doesn't actually appear anywhere until somebody actually observes it. In other words, the walls of a room are not really there until you look at them. When you're not looking at them, they return to their hyper-state. They could be where you last saw them, or they could be in Tibet. It might be many trillions upon trillions upon trillions to one, but scientists know there is a very faint chance that those walls are not there. Next time you look, they may be on the road to Tibet.

Considering the fact that solidity is created by observation, the ego intuitively knows that, so it requires observers to make it feel solid. The rock star, for example, needs observers, minders and body guards and a massage therapist, and agents and promoters and limousines, and they've got a gang of seventy people that travel around with them, observing them, making them special. "Yes sir, no sir, what do you want?"

In that specialness, the ego seeks to raise itself up, and what it is trying to do primarily is to distance itself from the destiny of humanity. The destiny of common people that are unimportant, let's say, for example, is to die. The more important a person is, the further they are from death. Because unimportant people, in countries where human life is not respected much, if a guy dies in the street, you step over him. Therefore, the destiny of a common man is to just be plowed under and die; whereas, the ego of the ivory tower is the ego of somebody who is terribly special and highly observed.

They go through this illusion of importance, the illusion of immortality. They create for themselves this idea that they are immortal. That is why Hollywood stars go through surgery and Botox and transplants and hairdos and breast lifts and whatever they do, because it creates this illusion, *I am an immortal, and that's what the ego wants to do.* It wants to become a demigod, to reach immortality, and one of the ways that it reaches immortality is to create observers. As I've stated, the observers feed the ego, the electricity, the tower goes up, and so the ego feels it's distanced from the destiny of humanity.

In many ways, in the journey beyond enlightenment, we don't seek to acquire any *new* energy because we've got massive amounts of energy. It's just that when the ivory tower isn't being held up and sustained by our concentration, we naturally come down. When we land on the grass, so to speak, it's known as the lunatic on the grass in these old writings. In other words, the lunatic on the grass is basically the lunatic that fell off the top of the ivory tower. Then he or she starts to go sideways and that's where all the perception is.

I've introduced the transverse wave of light, the zigzag wave that is going at 90 degrees to the forward motion of light. It's in that zigzag wave that you're connected to all of humanity. So you could say the forward motion of light is the ego in the ivory tower, zooming along, miraculously, at 300,000 kilometers a second, and the zigzag motion of light, the sideways motion of light, is our empathy, our feminine spirit. It's the yin compared to the forward yang. It's where we automatically join with humanity, and in that joining, we join into what psychoanalyst Carl Jung called the *collective unconscious*, but we also joined into the force field of the mirror self, which is the force field of the etheric.

You are connected to everybody; you can feel their pain. When you start to touch that empathy, it's an incredibly glorious experience, but also it creates an enormous compassion inside of you. Because rather than seeing somebody as a hard-nosed businessman who perhaps is rather predatory, you see them as a wounded child who is scared, who is grabbing all the toys like he did when he was three. In that empathy, you do see and you can feel the pain of humanity.

I have to tell you that empathy sometimes is tragic. You can sit in the lobby of the hotel and you can just observe the pain because you are watching slaves; you are watching human slaves who are being whipped by their egos. They have been whipped to perform; they have been whipped to succeed, to earn money, to consume way more than they ever need. You are basically watching a slave ship. You are watching men and women shackled to the floor of a slave ship, and they are walking through the lobby, and you can empathize with their pain. Of course, if they talk to you, then you can perhaps suggest that they don't do it anymore, but all torment is self-inflicted.

I suppose I would say that in the empathy, it's love, but it's more than love, because you are their pain, their pain is your pain. In other words, the world can't end until they feel okay. The world can't end until every single person is made well. You are connected. So in that connection, you can't get away from the fact that they are hurting, and I think the important thing about other people's pain is that you can't buy it, and you definitely can't make yourself responsible for it. The wise sort of fringe dweller spiritual warrior knows that they are not their brother's keeper. They are not here to interfere.

The greatest love that you can offer another human is to let them go; to let them be is to make them right. Love them as they are, even though you know that they are about to go over a cliff, psychologically. We can't buy their pain, but that doesn't mean that you don't have an empathy for it, but then the converse is true. Where you see people celebrating, people who are very light-hearted, you pick up on their joy.

It is important to guard that imprint of what you are, to guard it to become disciplined with it so that when you are ratty and crabby and upset, you have got to look at why you are tormenting yourself. Ask what's going on that's making you feel like this, and try to change that imprint. Don't blame others. People might say, *Oh, it's my husband that's making me upset.* It's not your husband. He is who he is, and he's probably just a little boy. Let him be. It's your reaction to him that's making you upset. It's your reaction to life.

When you are making other people a scapegoat for your own discomfort, then you realize that you are projecting your shadow. You are in your shadow play. When you think you are going to your most righteous, most preserved state, that is when you are going to your complete darkness. It's your ugliest state. Because if you say, *So and so is dark*, what you are saying is, *I'm dark*.

We need to take responsibility. You would ameliorate that situation by saying, *Look, I know I am calling you dark, Harry, I am sorry, I love you. It's actually my own darkness that's coming out today, because I am dog tired.* Or *it's my darkness that's coming out today, because I am really pissed off, and I have had a hard day at work.* Or *it's my darkness coming out because I feel my energy dropping, and I think I am getting a bit of flu.*

Mainly, it's the act of being responsible because I can't make you angry. I can do things that might stimulate your anger, but you have to agree to be angry. I could do things that were really irritating, but you could say, *Wow, that's just you being you. He's kind of been a bit foolish. He's a bit weak today, he's a bit dishonest.* Therefore, when people rip you off, you can be angry that they ripped you off. Or you could say, *They are weak, you know; they better have the money, they probably need it.*

What can people do when they can realize that the imprint they make today is the pain that they will receive in three weeks' time—or the glory? For example, in road rage, you might be seething because people are cutting you off in traffic. You might eventually think, *I don't want to drive because this is potential for a disaster.* But, of course, not driving isn't the answer, because that's just letting go of your responsibilities or letting go of a tool that is useful because it gets you around the town.

The answer is to remember that all road rage comes from your own self-importance. Because if six other people want to get in line in front of you, you could say, "This is a beautiful day for waiting," and you let them go first.

It's only your self-importance that thinks this place in the line for the traffic light is your place and you are an important person and have got to get there at 9:10. But, in fact, you are not an important person. You are a divine, eternal, spiritual person who can wait in line forever. So if a hundred cars want to go ahead of you, let them. All the road rage, in fact, is not the person that's raging, but the person that is being raged at, and usually what happens is the road rage is some other rage that you had three weeks ago. Maybe you were raging at your kids for nothing. Okay, they left a few toys on the carpet, and you put your foot on the truck and fell over. So you raged at the kids for an hour about how messy they are, and then a month later, some guy's raging at you waving a gun at you on the freeway, but you say, *Oh,*

I was so innocent driving along the freeway, like the angel of mercy. When in fact that's just your own rage coming back.

In other words, you are a transmitting and receiving station of etheric downloads and imprints. Some are graphic, some are mental, and some are in the buzz that I spoke of. There's so much information that you may not be aware of as yet. A wonderful story in your soul is unfolding from deep within. You should never worry about where you will go and how you will get there. You will know, trust, and learn to trust, and the more you are aligned to a soft world and a spiritual way, the more you will see it come miraculously into your life.

We are all in the morph, and it is in us and in the record of your life so far and in your future possibilities in all their glory, even though that future may be somewhat hazy right now. We are all in a hologram, and possibly the whole universe is a hologram, and you are in my molecule, and I am in your molecule—that might be a critical realization one day. You are in a loop. What goes around comes around. We all have a rudimentary understanding of that, as we experience it day to day, but what is the technical reason for energy and karma coming back to us?

Your mind imprints your etheric bio-photons, and they go out as light from you, and they imprint reality around you. They especially imprint other people who are mainly made of water; those people will react negatively or positively toward you. As you react to their reaction, you pump more subtle feelings into your mirror self, adding to your stored memories, and through these stored memories, your mirror self changes. It tends to drift back and forth in the mirror world to parts that reflect your current state. It will go from sacred, happy, and blissful, to angry and hellish.

Gradually, the mirror self starts to pump energy back toward you here in the physical world, and that returning energy reflects in your body and your mind. The return energy is what you put out emotionally and mentally into your etheric, weeks ago. Eventually, you take your own stuff back as an energy hit in your physical body.

Overcome Fear

All disease starts in the mind, traveling through our etheric and on into the mirror world where it solidifies and bounces back, developing speed all the while to come back to us several weeks later. A lot of the work comes initially from fear. It's weird that our evolution has so much to do with processing fear. Here are a few etheric moves for processing and transcending fear.

First, you should never be ashamed of your fears. We humans are small and fragile, poised as we are in an enormous universe. Any one of a dozen things can take us out at an instant. Yet overcoming fear is part of learning to love, for we cannot love when we are afraid. Fear leaves no space for such positive emotions, so it swamps your mind and closes your heart and your etheric goes gray and dull looking.

The more open you become, the more vulnerable you are. It's a test. By letting go and becoming more and more open, you allow yourself to be open to danger, uncertainty, rip-offs and, of course, ridicule. Can you live in the restrictive environment of the ego's fears and the rules they will impose upon you? Can you truly express yourself as a complete person, a spiritual person, if you don't take risks and go for it? The only way forward in my view is bit by bit as fast as you can accommodate your insecurity. Here are a few ideas with some etheric moves, which you might find helpful.

Most persistent low-grade fear is not due to psychological issues or a poor state of well-being. It is often only due to dehydration because most of us don't drink enough water. The water in alcohol and beverages doesn't count. We need about eight 8-ounce glasses of clean water a day, which is just less than three liters. Otherwise, body cells become dehydrated, and fear and insecurity increase dramatically.

Action Step: Why dehydration causes fear and anxiety, I don't know. We just observe that it does. Most people would not be scared or depressed if they were better hydrated. If you rehydrate your body, you will see a dramatic improvement in days. Drink eight large glasses of water a day and take three lecithin tablets spread out during the day. You can find lecithin at the health food shop. You can take lecithin in granules if you would like, instead of the capsules.

The lecithin helps the uptake of water in the cells, and you will notice a substantial reduction in your levels of anxiety after about three days. In total, it takes about three weeks to completely rehydrate the body properly. Once you have done that, remember to keep your water intake up and increase it whenever you feel fear and insecurity creeping back in.

The hydration discipline is so simple. It gets rid of most low-grade fear, and it helps with mild depression. As you discipline the ego and begin to control it, your life becomes less fearful. Meditation helps a lot for it's the only way to properly discipline the mind and stop it thinking so much. The less you worry, the more open you become. Then the more open you become, the more etheric light is infused within you. The less energy you waste and burn, the more transcendental you will feel, and so the less insecure you will be.

Most fear comes from suffering from low energy, which may be mental or physical. Confrontation, for example, sets up fear of collapse. That is why the unknown poses such a problem for many people. They worry that they might not be able to sustain themselves financially, physically, or emotionally in different circumstances. However, when you are powerful, you can express that power wherever you go. Changing locations and circumstances means little to you, for you are strong within yourself.

Action Step: If you are insecure, do this. Exercise every day for twenty minutes if you can. Even gentle exercise like walking is better than no exercise. If you don't exercise, you will get scared. Remember, extra fat in your body is stored fear or stored pain. It's ancient memories in your flesh. Certainly, we all put on a bit of weight in middle age, but you have to lose that by the time you get to your late fifties or early sixties, as there aren't many old fat people.

To be healthy in old age, you have to be normal and thin. I would be the last person to offer you a weight loss diet. I am sure you are fed up with all those fads and the hype that surrounds them, except to say that all the transcendental adepts that I know, the true morph warriors, are almost all vegetarians, as they don't like to kill to survive, and they don't like to ingest the fear that is in the animal's body meat. Most of them live substantially on raw food diets.

When food is raw, it's alive, and it has light in it. I am not an expert on these things, but I have cooked food in the winter when it's cold, but I do go on a diet that has a lot of raw food as the spring comes along. If you want to study up on raw foods, check out the books on super-foods by David Wolfe.

Action Step: Try to rest and sleep. So many modern achievers and high-action modern families suffer from sleep deprivation. Sleep and rest whenever you can and allow yourself at least one hour a day of quiet time to ponder your life and your strongest moves. Not having time to yourself can make you anxious.

Life requires us to be brave. Nurturing yourself and resting and being calm and in control develops security and personal strength. Also, having less responsibility and activity helps. You can soon lose yourself and become fearful if your life is too cluttered. I know many people who sold up and quit the life of the yuppie world, and they took their little suitcase and floated off to discover themselves. Of course, if you have families and children, you may not be able to do that, but maybe you can adjust your life to be less active.

Often we work hard to pay bills, and in the act of working, we create more bills. We buy things. But if you think about it, everything you own, in the end, winds up owning you. I can't remember who said that, but he or she is right. Not long ago I took my suitcase and headed out on a journey of 60,000 miles. I was away for three and a half years, and I spent a lot of that time on a bed watching the morph, but I learned more in that time than the whole rest of my life put together. Choices can carry you beyond stress and fear to redemption.

I learned a lot about the nature of terror and fear as a firewalking instructor. My associates and I walked about 8,000 people over the years. It was interesting how people handled the unknown of walking barefoot across hot stones. I would tell people just before they walk the fire that the ego would quit and seemingly leave, and that they would walk as if in a dream, often not recalling what happened. I tell people that because of the altered state that fear puts one in, that they would probably want to walk the fire twice. Few of them ever believed me. Yet on every firewalk we facilitated, about 65 percent of the participants would go over the fire a second time.

Life is often like the moment just before a firewalk. Fear wipes your consciousness, and you enter into a self-induced hypnotic state. Life passes you by; years can go by without your ever realizing the true you. Time flies when you are stuck.

Awareness is a gift granted to the courageous. You can't get rid of fear entirely, but you can come into control of your mind, and by disciplining yourself you feel more confident and more secure. It's not hard. Fear is a bad habit for most people—one that they can learn to control.

Action Step: If you suffer from nightmares, stop eating protein after about six in the evening, as most nightmares come from food, especially heavy protein. Just eat very lightly early in the evening, no heavy stuff like steaks and so on.

Here are a few etheric tricks that will also help you when you are really scared. One, make a fist and thump yourself fairly forcefully in the sternum, center chest, as many times as it takes to change the energy of the heart chakra. That opens it to more energy. Don't punch too hard—the sternum is quite fragile—but just hard enough to effect change.

Two, put your thumb and your first two fingers together on both hands, and tap both your cheeks simultaneously an inch or so below your eyes. Do this vigorously and quickly. There's a meridian there, and tapping changes the energy flow.

Three, put one hand over the other and place them both over your navel, pressing inward gently. You can do this lying down facing up if you wish. Etherically, fear flows out of the solar plexus. It gushes out like rain through a storm pipe. Putting your hand over your navel stems the loss of energy. The less energy you lose, the more calm you become.

Four, lock the fingers of your hands together and place them on top of your head across the middle, covering your crown chakra, and pull your arms downward, pressing yourself down into the ground. That action pulls your etheric back down and inhibits your imagination from flying off the handle. If a child is a bit hysterical, just place your hand firmly on the top of its head and press down. Hold the other hand lightly against the child's navel pressing inward, both hands working together simultaneously. The hand on the top of the head is good for calming kids and getting them off to sleep.

You can also touch them etherically at a distance as long as you can see them. Imagine yourself with an extended arm. See yourself reaching out etherically and place your etheric hand on the child's head mentally, using the authority of your will. Imagine yourself pressing down on the child. In fact, I use this technique quite a bit when lecturing to stop babies in the audience from crying.

Five, if you are panicky, or feel you are too speedy and out of control with anxiety, lie down with your head to the north and your feet to the south on the ground, in the dirt is best. Try to get as much of your skin in contact with the ground as possible. If conditions permit, take off all or most of your clothes. Then visualize pushing the fear down through your body into the ground, anchoring it by saying, *Mother Earth I am giving you back this fear of mine.*

Another alternative is to allow natural running water to run down your spine. You could lie down in a stream. The water trick also works when you feel your energy dropping as if you are getting the flu. When I was traveling on the road as a lecturer, I used to get in the shower. Once it was nice and warm, I would flip it quickly to the cold water and let it run down my spine and then go back hot and cold, hot and cold, and do it four to six times. See if you can stand it at least three times anyway.

In conclusion, all fear is the fear of loss or the fear of death. Not necessarily physical death, but the death of things that we are familiar with such as our relationships or our job or perhaps a situation that's familiar that is about to change. Start to train your mind, if you have not done so already, to see change as beneficial and necessary. Nothing persists forever. So don't hold on, be prepared to release aspects of your life and allow the law of flow to come into your life.

What Did You Do for This Planet?

Do you see where we are going with all of this? It's an uncoupling process. First, you look at your inner self and the existence of the mirror world self, and then you see the clusters you are in and how they hold you, and you glimpse the possible liberation of your soul.

One of the important questions we came upon as we went that way is how will you imprint reality as you go along? What is your purpose here? That can be answered by, *I work and pay rent, and then I work some more, and I rush to accumulate things until I have no more energy, and then I'll die.* But what kind of purpose is that?

Most people are just taking up space and generating pollution. It makes you wonder how long the soul of this planet is going to stand for that. So you can see how in developing a higher purpose you develop a spirituality beyond the mundane. It seems to me that the purpose of life should be first to use your income to buy experiences for yourself. You have knowledge and experiences that you can share with others, and then, surely, the main purpose of your life is to be of service, not just service to any children and family members that you might be caring for, but service to humanity, or service to the animals or service to this planet in some way.

You see, as I said before, all that will count for anything when you die will not be how many mortgage checks you paid. Or how much money you left your family. But what did you do for this planet? Did you serve? How much did you love them and help them? Through service we operate our heart space, and we install energy in the hologram of life. It's a bridge we build for others and ourselves.

In service, it might seem that you're supporting others, but, in fact, you're learning to honor and serve the eternity within yourself. It's a form of remembering, a higher remembering that is imprinted in your soul, and there are signposts all the way, taking us back to what we already know in our ancient memory. We're raised to think that this life is all about us, and how cozy and comfortable we can become. But if you think that life is just about you, then you've been surely misled. You haven't gotten to a real sophistication in your comprehension of things.

In the journey beyond enlightenment, what we're looking at is the paradox of the fact that the more things you have, the more you're in prison. Everything you own in the end winds up owning you, and that's a fact. You buy a fancy car, you can't drive it. I used to have a Rolls Royce, but you couldn't drive the bloody Rolls Royce because you couldn't park it, because somebody might scratch it. If you scratch a Rolls Royce, it's $1,000 to get a door painted, maybe more.

I couldn't have dinner worrying about my car on the street. But I was young and foolish when I had that car. I should have gone out with my car keys and scratched the bloody door myself. That way, I wouldn't have had to worry about having a scratched Rolls Royce, because it was already scratched.

Let's go back to the analogy of pop singers. They create this ivory tower, then they've got these mansions, but then they fear loss. Now they need bodyguards who are charging them $800 a day, and they need dogs and surveillance, and they need huge fences, and they need to protect themselves, and then you can't just ring them up because they're terribly important. You have to ring their agent in New York.

There's a wonderful story of an opera singer who is in a limo, and she's known for being unbelievably capricious and sort of edgy and a sort of mad diva causing trouble. She was riding in this limo in LA, and it was too cold in the back, so she phoned her agent in New York, to call the opera house to call the limo company to call the driver to tell him to change the air conditioning because she couldn't tell him from the backseat to the front seat. It's like an urban legend, and I've been told that it's true. Such self-importance. But that's the epitome of the ivory tower.

You may not as yet understand that this life has very little to do with you, except in the marginal sense that you have to care a little for your upkeep day to day, but that may only amount to a cup of rice each day. After that your real journey starts elsewhere. Focusing on you and your needs is not the be-all and end-all of your life's purpose. You may have had an inkling of a proper purpose over the years. Spirit may have talked to you in quiet moments. The part of your mind that thinks it's running your life is laboring under a delusion.

Yes, the mind pretends to run your life, but that's all part of the con. It controls nothing, even though it will insist the opposite. Your life has nothing to do with your mind, even if you think it does. You can become part of something much bigger and more glorious once you give yourself away, and then you'll see it. I've often said that the spiritual journey through life is just four feet long. You travel one foot downward from your head to your heart, and three feet outward to embrace the first human you meet. That is the ivory tower coming down. Allow yourself a tactile contact with the reality of humanity—its soul so to speak.

Spirituality Is Empathy

In the end, it's all about deliverance, and that deliverance is more important than anything else in the world. You deliver yourself from forgetfulness, and then you deliver others that are drawn to you. For if you don't deliver them, who will? They don't have much of a chance without you. Think of that, they can't escape until you agree to help them escape.

Now you might think this deliverance business is a bit dodgy and wonder why you need it. And I'd say most people care little for deliverance, but that is mainly because they can't see what is waiting for them up the road.

We are surrounded by a world of dark energies, and they're all over this place looking to trap people. It's a war of control over the human mind. If too many people start remembering, those dark energies will lose their domination. Now I know some think that if they join one religion or another, they'll be instantly delivered, but that idea is fraught with problems. A religion could offer you the hope of an elitist deliverance, but no such thing exists. It's a bit of a ghoul's trap.

Spiritual seekers have the biggest ivory towers because they play to an elitism of us and them, and the us and them elitism says generally, we're special and chosen by God, the sage, the guru, the adept, to survive. We are the ones that will survive; the common man will not survive. So it's back to the ivory tower. We are the ones that have been made right by the will of God or by the holy book or by those sacred, and that makes us very different, very special, and that's why some spiritual groups sort of wear white clothes and a white diaper on their head. They wander around doing spiritual New Age things, but in that whiteness, they're really,

really dark because to distance yourself from humanity and to be elitist, and chosen, and special is fatal. It's part of the devil. You're not special.

There's nothing special about you, and yet we're all special in a sense. We're a child of God, and we're unique, but in effect, there's nothing special about me or you or anyone, and the idea that God will select one group of people over another is piffle, complete rubbish. Have you been selected by God to survive? No, you haven't, but if you have been, you're lucky.

Spirituality is empathy. That's all it is. It's an empathy with every single person you meet, and it's a special empathy with those people that you hate—those people who are really aggressive and violent and nasty. It's empathy for them.

Let me tell you a story about a man I know. He's Italian, in his fifties. He's very abusive, and he's been violent all of his life. He used to get involved in fights and he caused people pain. He loved beating people up, especially if they were smaller than he. He enjoyed inflicting damage. That was his thing in life.

He's also a sexist. He sees all women as placed on this earth to give him service and sexual pleasure, and he's always been a racist. He hates people who come from Africa or Asia, people with darker skin and he makes no bones about shouting out his racist ideas in the company of others. He's a Roman Catholic and religious, and he's also scared of death, but he believes his Catholicism will save him, and that he will go to heaven after his death because he has supported the church and attended mass.

But I think he may be up for a bit of a reality check. I feel for him because there's nothing I can do to change him. He likes his life. He's rich and powerful. He will never change his thinking. He knows I'm a spiritual writer, and sometimes he asks me about my philosophy, and I tried to tell him, but he's not the kind of person who would listen. I've known him for forty years. I don't see him often, but I tried to love him and not judge or criticize him, and I've never once ever told him he's wrong in the way that he deals with people. It's not for me to fix him, and I couldn't rescue him if I tried.

Strangely, this man has redeeming qualities, in that he's very funny and generous, and he makes a big show of splashing his wealth and paying for dinners and so forth, but that is his outer mask. His inner self is like something out of *The Sopranos*, and he's staying in the cluster until he dies. He's sort of transdimensionally abducted. He sees himself as holy and good, and yet his imprint on life is ugly and dark. You see his mirror self is trapped. It is as if he is possessed without ever knowing it. He lives in the section of the mirror world reserved for violent, racist Mafiosi that like to express their power by hurting others. They use intimidation to reign supreme over others. They think they're special, and power and money drives that illusion of elitism and specialness.

Once you comprehend the loop you're in, you get out and you watch how you're imprinting realities as you go along. You are a snowflake, a beautiful snowflake, or you are a dark picture of evil, polluting everything you touch and making people sick as you walk past them in the street. We live in a sea of energy.

If you put out a truly soft imprint, and you love the world, everything you touch, everything you breathe in, has the basis of remembering, and the next person who touches the same shopping cart, for example, will also begin to remember. It's the heart space or tone that you leave behind you everywhere you go that becomes a doorway for others. They sit on the same bench and their mind will drift and they will slide to a 90-degree world without knowing it, and suddenly they will hear faint sounds of their soul calling to them, asking them to step away from cold and tight and pain toward a freedom. They start to remember, and that's our function here in this world is to help people remember.

Thoughts Jump

How many times have you been thinking about something obscure, and the person next to you mentions the very thing you've been thinking about? Silent communication generally comes about when you're thinking in the direction of another person rather than concentrating inwardly toward your own thoughts and emotions. You have to set your mind to one side and concentrate on others. It's hard to stop your mind talking. It likes listening to itself, but it can be done with a little bit of discipline.

Silent communication of the human soul can be in the form of prayers or silent affirmations for the well-being of others. Then there's the actual mental dialogue that is spoken in the direction of another person. It is a telepathic transfer of energy, and hopefully it is a silent dialogue that offers love and encouragement of some sort.

In Paris recently, I was watching a middle-aged lady walking into a café. She looked a bit stressed out. I asked her silently, *Are you afraid?* She turned toward me and nodded. I asked, *Are you sick?* She shook her head. I breathed love into her heart. She passed behind me and took a seat. Minutes later, a tall man in his seventies came by; he looked in pain. I asked silently, *Do your lungs hurt?* He grabbed his shirt with his right hand. He looked at me helplessly. It was a look of a small child begging a grownup for assistance. I told him silently, *Drink lots of water, clean water. It's the key to everything.*

As I was walking through the customs hall in Philadelphia's airport, the official stopped me. He wanted to look inside a metal flight case I was carrying. I touched him on the side of the head mentally and projected a soft, warm feeling. I said mentally, *It's safe. I need to go now. Thank you.* He hesitated and pointed to the case as if requiring that I open it, and again I said silently, *It's safe. I need to go now.* He pulled his hand back and asked, "Are those computers?" And I answered audibly, "Yes, sir." He waved me through.

When you talk silently to people, look at their right temple and blank your mind. You just tap them with your thoughts, like reaching out with your hand to touch them at the side of the head, blink once as the thought goes across, or expel a short breath. The more silent and subtle the better. The harder you try, the less effective you are. Be soft and subtle.

Morphic resonance is the language of force fields interacting with each other. Your brain is a complex force field that stores and receives information in the form of wave packets. We are a holographic brain inside a holographic universe. There's no distance between anything. We're all connected; we're inside the same global mind, the global subconscious.

Once you know you can talk silently, then start doing it and remember to watch and see if they twitch, as those twitches will tell you that there are pulses coming through to them from the mirror world. Sometimes they don't twitch but they move their eyes upward. That means they're entering a mild trance at about 4 to 7 cycles a second. If the incoming pulse that is coming to them is pain related, they might wince. What you will learn is that if you ask a question of them, they will often show you the answer. Like the man with the bad lungs who grabbed his shirt.

You watch their lips carefully and you watch their eyes. The telltale signs are often in the lips and the eyes, and you will soon see that you can read people easily. Try for the obvious first. Anger is easy to spot, as is arrogance. Remember, arrogant people tilt their heads back as if the nasty smell of lesser beings is under their nose. Violent people have a madness in the eyes; they give off a strange bend in the etheric. And if you ever see people who have white under their pupil, between the pupil and the lower eyelid, that is often the sign of a true psychopath. It is known as *sanpaku* (danger).

I used to teach that to my kid and his mates to increase their awareness in case anyone came into the playground that looked like that. If we could walk in the street, I could show you all of it in several hours or even less, maybe, but you can teach yourself. I did. No one showed me. I learned by watching, and as a person passes, reach out etherically extending your arm and grab a small molecule from their center chest area, and pull that back toward yourself real fast and blank your mind. Don't be overly influenced by what clothes they're wearing or how they look. As the etheric energy comes back to you, ask yourself how does this feel?

When you go into a restaurant or café, ask *How does this feel?* This place and the memory of the walls will talk to you. *How does this feel?* It's always in the feeling.

In the etheric state, you have the ability to step into the subtle energy of another person. For example, I talk about moving your etheric, your subtle body, out of your physical body, turning that subtle body to face you. And then stepping backward with your etheric into the physical body of another person that you're talking to, for example, like dropping backward into them. Visiting another person etherically in this way is okay, providing you're not manipulating them, or making them do things that they don't want to do. It's a way of joining them, being with them, concentrating on that person.

In the end, concentration is a form of love. When you're focused upon a person, you're in the act of loving them. This dropping backward into another person's energy is like the tapping, except they are close to you at the time, not across the street, and you're only ever in there for a few seconds, but while you're in there, you can hear the sound of their soul. You can hear and feel who they are and what they're feeling at that very moment. You have enormous power. Some of it lies in and beyond your stored pain, and some of it is here right now, and some of it is only available from time to time; it just flips through when needed.

It's only at the very end, many decades from now, that all the spiritual warriors and fringe dwellers that have the remembering, each will decide, and they will have to step across and stay there and not come back, or they can choose to stay here as teachers and healers and wise people, but no one knows what world they will inherit. It may not be the world we know today. But once you are bigger than the dark, then you are safe.

4

The Inner and Outer Matrix

Truth in the spirit world exists around each one of us. Embracing true reality, both the pleasure and the pain of it, is the only path to true spiritual freedom.

To help you fully understand my concept of this inner and outer matrix, I turn to the movie *The Matrix* to describe both literal and metaphorical realities about the spiritual terrain in which we live, either consciously or unconsciously. Ideally, you might prepare yourself by viewing the film, but here's a short synopsis of the plot to prepare you for some of the ideas that I discuss in this chapter.

A computer software programmer named Thomas Anderson, played by Keanu Reeves, leads a secret life as a hacker under the alias Neo. A series of unusual events brings him into contact with a group of people led by Morpheus, played by Laurence Fishburne. Morpheus explains to Neo that the matrix is a false reality and invites him to enter the real world. Morpheus offers Neo two pills: the red pill will answer the question, *What is the matrix?* by removing him from it, and the blue pill will simply allow life to carry on as before. As Neo reaches for the red pill, Morpheus warns Neo that all he is offering is the truth, nothing more.

Of course, Neo takes the red pill, and his life is never the same. There in the real world, Neo discovers that the year is not 1999, but about 2199 and that humanity is fighting a war against intelligent machines. In order to deny the machines their power source, solar energy, the humans scorch the sky. The machines responded by making use of human beings themselves as an energy source. It turns out that the world which Neo has inhabited since birth, the matrix, is an illusionary simulated reality construct of the world of 1999 developed by the machines to keep the human population docile while they are connected to generators and their energy is harvested.

Morpheus with the other free humans works at unplugging humans from the matrix and rescuing them. Morpheus has rescued Neo from the matrix because he believes that Neo is the one who has been prophesized by the Oracle to "hail the destruction of the matrix and the war and bring freedom to our people."

Morpheus believes that Neo has the power to free humankind from its enslavement through complete mastery over the matrix. Neo, along with the other members of Morpheus's group, is initially skeptical, but Morpheus teaches him to bend or break the rules of the matrix, to subvert the operation of the normal laws of physics. Neo also forms a close personal relationship with a female member of the group, Trinity.

Inside the matrix, the humans are pursued by a group of self-aware programs called *agents* having incredible martial arts skills and capabilities beyond those of humans. Their most powerful skill is their ability to jump between bodies, enabling them to take over any person who has not been disconnected from the matrix. Ultimately, Neo develops the ability to defeat the artificial intelligence within the matrix, and begins the process of restoring humans to their rightful place as the sentient species on the planet.

Domination of Our Unseen World

In the *Matrix* film, the character Morpheus talks about fields upon fields that form invisible layers of control over humanity. What is incredible is that in the four years since I started watching the morph, I began to see those layers of transdimensional control Morpheus talks of.

Humanity is dominated from an unseen world, under the influence of a matrix of unseen beings. We are only now able to see the truth of it. If you tell people that humans are not the most powerful beings here on Earth, and they don't really dominate, people would think you're nuts, and they would probably ridicule you and say it's not possible. Yet that is exactly the truth that has been cleverly hidden from us for tens of thousands of years.

What Neo saw in *The Matrix*, he couldn't hack. I'll tell you a bit about the dark forces I met up with and then I'll tell you about the light ones, and that will give you a balanced view.

Remember, people's fear of the dark is a deliberate ploy, one that has been engineered to make sure you never escape to the feminine side, to the arms of the goddess. The idea is you will remain in the yang, too terrified to move, and that the dark will rule the world forever. People are preprogrammed to react. Hollywood has helped sell the fear, and in doing so, they have further trapped humanity.

To become free, you have to go the other way. Love the dark, leave the war-like yang, embrace the feminine, and don't be a wimp and set yourself free. There's an inner and outer matrix of control, and once you know what to look for, you will see how to fashion a spiritual escape from the grand lies imposed on you that hold you back. The New Age and certain religions try to deny the dark, hoping it will go away, and that denial only allows the dark to become ever more powerful, and to hide ever more in the minds of people and become stronger.

Part of our mission here in this life is to expose the transdimensional beings and the mechanism of control and to teach our brothers and sisters not to be scared anymore.

Normally, you wouldn't need to know any of this information, and I could just not mention it. I could give you the cheesy version—rah-rah living in the light, stick your head in the sand, bums up, heads down, everything will be fine. But if I did that, it would mean that I didn't care for you and your soul, and it would also say that I didn't care if you had the proper knowledge or not. That would be rather callous of me.

All these things we know have come from watching them in the screen of the morph. How would my frail soul rest if I knew I'd sold you a crock and not told you how to make it or what to expect. I have to presume that you're strong, and that you truly are going to try for the journey beyond enlightenment through the side door I talked about. To do so, you have to have the knowing of things, and knowing things helps you be less vulnerable.

Down the Rabbit Hole

If I had to summarize the whole journey, it is understanding that the things that you've done in the past have created struggle and pain, and they've also created the confusion of not knowing, and so it's in the turning around and going the other way that, first of all, you disengage from the knowing that wasn't correct or the misinformation that you were offered, and you begin moving toward your authentic self. It knows where the door is, because it's beyond the door. So it can show you.

This journey is not so much acquiring any new dogma, but it's liberating yourself, really sitting down one day and admitting that it hasn't worked. If your life is working fantastically and you really happen to like your ivory tower, it wouldn't be for me to change that. This is for those people who intuitively believe there is a force beyond what they see day to day, a miraculous force, a force that is in essence the God force. This force

is more than willing to show you when you stop playing with your Lego set in building this funny little wob-
bly life with all the pain that is involved, that there is
a place that initiates have gone for hundreds, perhaps
thousands of years, and they've gone out through the
side door. That's the next evolution.

It's very much a journey for those people or those
fringe dwellers who are fed up with listening to the
same old stuff, who are fed up with rah-rah, trying to
incorporate the rah-rah in their life, finding that after
two or three weeks, the rah-rah isn't there, and then
experiencing more endless ripples in your consciousness. It's like this: you go up the hill, you go down the
hill, you go up the hill, you go down the hill. The ripples are just where the human consciousness has been
folded over, over and over and over like little folds in a
blanket, which humanity has to sort of travel across to
get out, and, of course, nobody's gotten out going the
other way. It's never been done.

The journey beyond enlightenment is not a journey
forward or upward or joining anything. It's rather the
act of walking away and realizing that enlightenment
might be a good thing for certain people. Certain people need to stop at the crossroads and become a great
holy man or a great medicine woman, but if you're truly
enlightened, you aren't going to mess with that because
it's too rinky-dink. What you really want to do is go back

to the arms of God, and the arms of God are through that side door.

If you ask why should you join me on this journey and head out into an unknown terrain, the only thing I could say to you is that you don't have to but the world is changing very, very rapidly, and if you don't grow and perceive and liberate yourself, it will be liberated from you anyway. You can stay where you are, but the towers are coming down. In the next ten or fifteen years, you will see nothing but the collapse of the system.

Therefore, you can sit there and insist on it, and love it and care for it and paint your ivory tower for as long as you want to paint it, but one day, it'll fall anyway. It's really a matter of whether you want to leave now on this gentle, sacred journey. If yes, the journey involves a certain amount of unknown, of facing up to what is real. Or do you want to sit there and watch the tower taken from you forcefully? That's your choice. If you say you'd like to sit here and build an ivory tower and put diamanté studs on it, I'd say fine. I mean, I wouldn't judge that ever. It's not for me to judge. Everybody must choose.

It's like Morpheus says in *The Matrix*. You take the red pill, and you see how far the rabbit hole goes. In effect, the rabbit hole is the side door. Or you take the blue pill and you wake up in your bed, and you believe whatever you want to believe. When he said that, he wasn't being callous, he was empathizing with Neo. He was saying, *Look, bro, if you don't want to go down the rabbit hole, don't go. You can return to your life, your ivory tower, your bed, and remain in that place, but the world is changing.*

The world is going to change dramatically—the most change that history has ever seen in any short period of time—and that changing is upon us right now.

The Dual Nature of the Transdimensional World

Look at it like this: next to our manipulated world of media and hype and loads of people selling you the illusion of the up escalator, taking you the wrong way, there's a forest. Beyond the forest is a heaven. In the forest are millions of beings just like on Earth, cute little etheric beings, like fairy folk. A quirky way of looking at it is to say that the celestial worlds are surrounded by darkness; you have to cross the bog of stench before you get to the castle of the holy grail. This is the journey of the initiate, and this is the journey that has been taken by all since the beginning of time.

Here's the background of it all in more depth. In the fifteenth and sixteenth centuries, mystics spoke of the fields, invisible spheres of influence that surround Earth and humanity. They were known as the sphere.

The sphere theory of medieval times is very interesting because humanity is inside a bubble, and that bubble is formed because we live in a physical universe that is made up of matter that has subatomic particles that spin twice. It's the double spins symmetry of our solid world that creates the bubble or the sphere that we are trapped in.

Think of a revolving door at a hotel. You're in the lobby, and you know there is a celestial world out in the street. So you enter the revolving door and it spins very fast twice, and it plunks you back in the lobby, back in 3-D. You never got out. That's why we humans are stuck. The only way out is not trying to force your way out through the revolving door. Instead, you have to go sideways and walk through the wall beside the door.

Meanwhile, loads of unseen guards are in the lobby making sure you don't try and get out or even think about it. How we did it was using the morph as a lens. A pal and I traveled through the Shadowlands for three and a half years; it's like watching a movie on a screen except you're watching the screen, on the one hand, and you're in the film at the same time.

That is the dual nature of these transdimensional worlds. While moving through, we discovered the secrets of the inner and outer matrix of control. It's quite technical, so I'll keep it as simple as possible.

The outer matrix contains all the transdimensional beings that seem to be outside of us. I use the word *seem* because all of reality is outside of you and inside of you at the same time. It's the duality once again. This is because your perception of reality is only an electrical impulse in your brain. So the city street may be outside of you in one sense, yet the only way to experience it is inwardly inside you. But in the context of the outer matrix, we say that the outer matrix includes all those dark beings that appear to be outside and beyond oneself.

You have to realize that it's very much like in the film *The Matrix* when Neo took the red pill. His reality was stripped away. What he thought was real—the noodle shop on the corner—became unreal, and when he came back from that journey, he had to remake himself.

A Healing Journey

Yes, it can be scary when all the things that you believe, you suddenly come to not believe anymore; but, in many ways, that is the return to the authentic you, the uncluttered you, away from the fake you that was given so much misinformation. To return to the uncluttered you, which has more of the real information, you do need a sophistication and a certain sort of stoic force of will to drive you forward just as Neo did in the film to drive himself forward. One could say it's the loss of innocence.

Innocence is beautiful, but there's a day when all of humanity will have to grow up. As you embark upon your own journey, you'll become much more sophisti-cated. For example, when people hear something they don't like, they prickle and get angry. If you're a sophis-ticated person, you can listen to all sorts of theories that you don't necessarily agree with without reacting.

For example, I went to a lecture by a famous scien-tist who talked for an hour and fifteen minutes about the Big Bang. I don't personally believe in the Big Bang, but I wasn't up for having a fight with a lecturer. I was really interested to hear why he believed in the Big Bang, and what his methodology was, and what his sci-ence was, and his reasons for believing in it. You may well disagree with some of the things that I've been saying, but as sophistication of self allows you to listen, once you go down this path through the hidden door that I have been speaking of, you will realize that they were just encumbrances that you took on that you bor-rowed from other people, books, various dogma of one kind or another.

You may be able to relate to times when you suf-fered a loss of innocence, for example, when you've dis-covered that your boyfriend or your partner has been unfaithful to you, or the day that you had to straighten up and go take your driving test. These are all moments on the path where you have to become a grownup, a real being, and this journey beyond enlightenment requires you to develop a metaphysical, spiritual, and psychological maturity. But in that maturity, you can't beat yourself up. You can't decry the situation because we have incarnated, as I said, in the third liberation into a world that is unjust, and there are all sorts of hidden forces that are hindering you, especially when you want to do something that's holy and good. Some of those forces that you think are outside of you that are hindering you are, in fact, manifestations of you hindering yourself.

Etheric beings in a parallel evolution that blip in and out of this one might seem jolly unlikely, but you may be familiar with the work of Jose Escamilla, the Hispanic American researcher who has photographed an etheric being he calls a *flying rod*. The flying rods are anywhere from a few inches long to fifty feet in length. They're fins that oscillate along their translucent etheric bodies, and they fly through the air at speeds of thousands of miles an hour. They also exist under water; they've probably always been here. They are part of the beings that are in the outer matrix.

Escamilla discovered the flying rods by accident when his video camera was left on one day. While editing his film, he noticed the strange flying rods zip into the frame, turn, and then fly out again, all in the space of a few frames. Jose Escamilla is innovative; you can find his work at www.roswellrods.com.

A friend of mine, Ralph Miller, runs a sacred temple in Brazil known as Heart of the Initiate, where they perform shamanistic ceremonies with a sacred brew found in the Amazon. Ralph told me that during the session that his temple's celestial beings frequently appear. They seem to dance and move about between the participants, healing people.

A friend of mine had a long-term injury in her hip from being a ballet dancer, and she told me that on her third temple journey, a group of women came to her from another world dressed with head scarves and they placed golden needles in her hip. And they also had certain herbal remedies with them that came from that inner space. When she came out of the session, many hours later, her hip was healed, and it has never troubled her since.

Medicine will go to another place soon, where healing the etheric body might be a major advance in all the mayhem of our world to final redemption. The healing rescue is underway.

The Perpetual Memory of the Mirror You

Using the *Matrix* film as an analogy once again, you could say that Zion is the world of humans, and the *squeegees* that attack the humans are the flying gulls and the etheric beings in the outer matrix, and Mr. Smith and his agents, devoid of warmth, are the discarnate beings of the inner matrix. They are programs inside the inner matrix. The beings of the inner matrix are inside the human mind, so they can morph into anyone, just as Mr. Smith can in the film. When they see your insecurity come up from within you as a wave pattern, and if that is seen to frighten you, then they come flying in in seconds to strike you emotionally and push you toward ruin.

Initially, Jung, in describing the collective unconscious, said that humanity was linked by archetypal symbols. We all understand mother, father life, death, joy, happiness, morning, night—these symbols are common to all humanity. But what he didn't understand was that this collective unconscious is actually a place; it's a dimension that is just as real as our physical dimension, and that is through this hidden door that I talk about.

In that place, there's an alternative you, a mirror you that looks exactly and precisely the way you look, and that mirror you contains all your feelings, and the memories in your subconscious mind. So your subconscious mind and your mirror you are one and the same. The mirror you in effect is your soul because your brain cannot contain the perpetual memory of you after death. At the moment of death the brain ceases. So without a mirror you, where all of your feelings and memories are stored, there would be no perpetual memory of you.

If there wasn't a mirror you, an alternative you in another dimension, there would be no eternal life, no life after death because everybody would go through all these trials and tribulations and lessons, and their brain would stop. The whole book would be burned, so to speak. It'd be like this incredible sacred text and somebody has burned the bloody thing at the end of eighty-two years. Life would be unmemorable, worthless if we can't remember what Harry did, or why he did it, and he can't remember.

Therefore, the mirror you in this other world exists to remember who you are after death. The mirror world contains everybody, because the strangest thing is that we're all in the mirror world right now.

If there are six billion humans here, there are six billion souls in the mirror world, right now. Imagine it as this vast dimension where it's as big as the planet Earth if not bigger, because the mirror world also includes all the identities of people that died last week, and last year and 100 years ago, probably. It's so vast, it has the souls of the dead, and the souls of those people that are alive.

The people who are alive are in the afterlife already, which is very strange to understand. And spirits evolve, they're in that mirror world, and you are in there as well. Even now, while you are alive, it's the afterlife and this life at the same time concurrently, and that mirror image of us sometimes known as the *doppelgänger* can operate in the mirror world without permission of your waking mind. It is as if your subconscious goes walk-about without your intellect having a say in what it is doing or where it goes. It is operating 24/7 regardless of whether you're awake or asleep. It's back to the idea of the authentic you because the mirror self is the real you, and the intellect is not the real you. It's just a con-coction of ideas and opinions, programs you inherited.

The mirror self is your real identity, and it is what you actually believe and feel about life, not what you pretend to believe. It's a construct of your innermost feelings. First you look at it, and then you decide to change it. Just knowing it and admitting to it is a huge step forward. Most people deny any knowledge of it. That leaves them vulnerable to the dark energies, but that is childlike and unsophisticated. The only safety is to look at the dark and see it as beautiful and trans-muted.

There is enormous power inside your darkness and with it you can resolve the authentic you and fuse it to the power of the physical, intellectual, emotional you that you operate from here on Earth. You can use this knowledge to unlock the matrix and escape, but it involves going the other way, almost everything is backward. It's in dark, really, the secret to everything.

When I tell people, they have to go the other way and embrace the shadow, they get edgy, or they don't believe me, but the dark in effect is not really dark at all. It is just stored pain or ancient pain, the sins of the father or mother that you inherited from hundreds of years ago.

There is a heroic beauty to it if you can resolve the pain, and then you can save others from going the wrong way. Maybe they don't have to go through the pain of the cluster as you broke it for them, and while the ancient pain may have hurt you, at times, it will now turn and empower you as your sword across the dark lands—once you love it, and you're not scared of it, and you can embrace it.

The stored pain within you is beautiful. Start to tell yourself that it was a learned response, a karma, an attitude you took that maybe didn't work, just a spiritual lesson. Once you're not scared of the dark, you are free.

Moving beyond the Imprint of Stored Pain

Action Step: Here's a shadow exercise to test yourself. Sit in a bar or a restaurant, a place where people go and relax and have a drink, and watch people come and go. Watch as the inner you responds in your mind.

Listen to the way the inner mind talks to you responding to the stimulus of the people coming and going. Watch where your mind goes and the kinds of things you concentrate on when you allow your subconscious impulses to come forward. Watch what conclusions you come to about others.

See how your intellect translates those pulses into a story—one that you tell yourself about a person you are watching. In effect, you are watching them while noticing the impulses coming from within you. Your inner self will go for their stored pain, especially any stored pain that looks the same as the pain in you. So watch as it judges people without knowing anything about them. Watch how you may silently react and growl if a person comes in that you don't like. Maybe they're wearing clothes that you don't agree with, maybe that talks to you of a childhood fear, or maybe it's the pain of early rejection. You reject the person you are watching because you've experienced rejection as a child.

If an overweight old man comes in with a pretty young girl on his arm, and she's in a short dress, you may react against them deciding he's a dirty old man, and she's a little gold digger. Of course you don't know the facts. He may be her uncle, but in watching the inner you, you see how it decides from stored pain. You might be jealous the girl is not with you, reflecting the stored pain of all the girls that ever turned you down is manifest, projected if you like, toward the old man walking in the door, who may be the sweetest, kindest man in the world. Yet you will wallpaper him in your pain, and that is how the pulses of the subconscious affect your imprint on the world. It's painted to look like the pain we suffered.

Soon you will see if you are human and warm in your heart or whether you are just a cold reptilian predator of humanity, a Mr. Smith in disguise. and as the girl in the red dress came through the door, did you look at the flowers she was carrying? Or was your subconscious attention pulled to her sexually?

Of course the girl in the short dress responded to her impulses and urges, maybe using sex to entice people or maybe she just seeks attention. Perhaps it's a money thing. She needs admirers to pay for her to have a good time, and then the ones that lust after her are in their shadow as human predators. They probably don't respect her as a woman or care for her soul. They just want her sexually.

As I said, we project pain on others through the etheric imprint we make, and those pulses may be driven by sexual desire, preference, snobbery, hate, affection, greed, indolence, and the desire for an easy ride. They're driven by endless factors that make up the inner you.

Sometimes the stored pain is manifested as inverted snobbery. That is when people who are socially or economically disadvantaged feel better than or more special than rich people, and so they hate high achievers. It's the angry revolutionary who detests the upper class because he or she is not included in the upper class. It's the communist proletariat, rising to kill the czar, because they admire the czar and they want to be like the czar. Inverted snobbery is the feeling of being superior to the systems, or to the people that reject you. It's very common in churches and spiritual groups.

The weird thing is, it's all backward. The people and the things you pretend to hate are those hidden parts of you that you are secretly in love with, or that you desire. Love is a form of concentration. Romantic love is concentrating on one person to the exclusion of others. To detest someone, you have to concentrate on them, projecting thoughts toward them. Usually the person you detest has something you admire or want, something that will help you understand your stored pain.

Why do people silently say no without necessarily knowing why they're rejecting you? Maybe you scared them with your unresolved pain. Do you repel them? Do you know? Maybe your weakness irritates them. Maybe you're too needy. It's a shadow trait to lean on others for financial and emotional support. Maybe you're too slimy, and the hidden predator leaks out. Maybe you're sneaky and loose with the truth. Maybe people instantly distrust you. Maybe they think you're after their money and maybe deep down they're right. Maybe there's a host of others following you, riding your pain, ready to jump across from you to others.

And maybe you're traveling about with a dark circus from the inner matrix, a victim of your own stored pain without ever knowing it. So that hidden darkness is there at every turn to make sure you don't get what you want. People believe in luck, and sometimes they think they are accident prone, but that is the simplistic explanation. Mostly, they have dark energies all around them.

The first defense, of course, is to have strong yang sentiments and go in the opposite direction. It's toward the goddess, the divine Mother, that starts in the imprint of your etheric energy. So your protection lies in understanding how you project your stored pain on others. It's a complicated subject, but once you know about it, you can teach yourself and it will change your life and empower you. You start to break away from the matrix. It is all about how you touch the world with your mind and how you breathe on them, and it's how you see everything and imprint everything to an invisible higher love.

Your pain is sorted and understood in the context of your life, and it's past now, and now you're looking to serve, to help others while they sort through their stored pain.

5

Your Role as a Magical Healer

The ivory tower I have discussed earlier is a construct of illusion held up by the electricity of the ego. A person who has arrived at the bottom of the tower in that they've fallen off the roof, or they've collapsed the tower, are known as the lunatic on the grass. Gradually, they heal from the trauma of the tower, and they let go and take to a spiritual path. Then they arrive sideways at what is called *zero point man* or *zero point woman*.

When the zero point man or woman walks close to the ivory tower of another, they can act as the magical healer without anyone ever knowing they did it. That is because they act as a grounding rod for the discharge of energy. It's a flash of electricity that comes off the tower, going through the zero point person and back into the ground. It's a form of deliverance.

Once you've sorted your fears a bit and brought your ivory tower down, then you have embraced a bit of humility, and you have thought about service and your purpose in life. Once you've made peace with your little brother or your little sister, and you have incorporated the memory of ancient pain into your shield, rather than having it victimize you, then you're ready to have a future as a magical healer because when you get to none, nil, zero, all you will ever have to do is touch things, or breathe on them.

Deepak Chopra told me once that there are still molecules of the breath of Jesus in every square meter of air that we breathe; your imprint stays forever, as far as I understand it. It's on the handle of a door you touched ten years ago, and once you silently change things in your heart, the symmetry will start going the right way. The imprint of the world will change, and soon you will see, it was all backward. You'll see that you've not come to raise people up—far from it.

One of your main functions will be to collapse people. That is the greatest gift of love you can offer another is to bring them down to the ground as that is where the sideways journey of the authentic self begins. No one ever made it going up. It's never been done. Now you may wonder what I mean, and I'd say remember the hotel lobby and the revolving door. Imagine there's a very important lady in the lobby, and she's rich and famous and she's on TV. She has a lot of observers and so a lot of electricity. She has heard that there is an immortality beyond the door. It'll probably be dressed as Islam or Buddhism or Catholicism or Zionism or Hinduism or green juice enemas up your Pilates-ism.

She's carrying a scaffolding pole that is fifteen feet high. It's all encrusted with diamonds. It's the symbol of her ivory tower. It won't go out of the revolving door and it won't go through the side door either, and she won't let go of the pole as her whole life is entrusted to it—and anyway she got it on Rodeo Drive and it cost her a slew of bucks. How will she ever throw it down and walk away and shuffle sideways? She can't.

She will die trying to get out of the revolving door by banging at it with a yoga mat, but the pole will be waiting for her in the mirror world because what you are at the moment of death is what you will see of yourself when you get up the tube and over to the other side. Deathbed recantations and last-minute apologies score for nothing. They're worthless. You are what you are. Whatever is contained in the authentic you—good, bad, ugly, or nice.

You remember, I said at the beginning of this book that when you get to where you're going, there's nothing, just blank nothing, an awesome bliss and eternal silence. It's very wide. It is the dimension of the zero point woman, the zero point man. They have no pole. They make walking slowly their pole. They have no medicine. They have no ism; they make shuffling sideways their ism. They have no power; they make absence of self their power. They have no special wisdom; they make remembering their only wisdom. They have no plan; they make forgetting to die their plan. They have no shield; they make their little brother or their little sister their shield. They have no physical body; they make a spark of the God force their body. They have no resolution; they make listening to the rain their resolution.

Can you see now? Does it feel different? Do you sense the power of backward and didn't you almost die crying at night in your bed, trying to go further and further forward and upward? It was a bit futile. Sorry about that, but it's our karma to go the wrong way. That is how this matrix is organized.

Remember, all information is heavily doctored and controlled, not just news and propaganda. But especially spiritual, metaphysical information, I'd say, has that kind of information that could allow you to escape and make a run for it, but how much of that type of information tells you, *Sideways, bubba, sideways, let's make a run for it*? Not much. Mostly, it signs you up for dogma, and it locks you in. There is something to join, and the next thing that happens is you hear this slight whooshing sound. They've put a vacuum cleaner hose on your wallet, slurp, slurp. It's all the power of the matrix for the most part, feeding off people, controlling them, scaring them, taking them up the garden path the wrong way.

Funny, sad, what can one do? You have to collapse the ivory tower or take the red pill and go the other way and see it for yourself. You have to pray and be humble, so the Great Spirit will assist you.

Great Visionaries Come from Dysfunction

In the journey of the magical healer, the alkaline healer brings everything back away from its acidity, away from its disease, back to sensible, and there's nothing wrong with a life that's in control and sensible. You can have things if you want, and you can even have bits of the ivory tower if you want, providing the ivory tower isn't controlling you. So the magical healer heals everything through their own example. For example, they're walking slowly while everybody's rushing. They're eating a small bowl of food when everybody else is pigging out. They are on a bicycle when everybody else is in their gas-guzzling SUVs.

We're not here to wag our finger against people, but the magical healer has this ability to return everything back to alkaline, back to the feminine. Acidity in the body is what creates disease. If you could have perfect alkalinity, you couldn't have disease. The magical healers are warm because they couldn't be the magical healer if they didn't have empathy for humanity. They naturally radiate a warmth—not a sort of cheesy "I love you" kind of warmth—but more just empathy, a relationship that is with everybody and everything, a caring, and in that warmth is the healing.

Cancer is a cold disease. Most of our diseases nowadays are cold diseases. They are diseases of a cruel cerebral mind, and a body that is overpolluted with smoke, drugs, fat, alcohol, and toxic substances. We suffer from cold diseases. In the olden days, people died from hot diseases. They died from fevers such as scarlet fever, the pox, typhoid. Our ancestors died of hot diseases, but our humanity today dies of cold diseases.

The ultimate magical healer would be the healer that never was aware that she'd healed anything, that at the end of her life, you would say to her, *Look, do you know that you've healed 100,000 people of cancer by just walking through the supermarket?* She would look back and go, *I did? I wasn't even aware that I'd done it.* In a way, that's the ultimate magical healer; and the less magical than that will be one who was aware, but they never asked for anything, and they never said anything; and then ever so slightly less magical than that would be somebody who has a shingle hanging out for appointments at $60 each.

The ultimate healing would be when you didn't know you had healed anybody. At the same time, the ultimate teaching would be when you never realize you've taught anybody anything. You were just at a fountain talking. I remember one night in England. I was in Glastonbury, which quite a mystical sort of New Age town, and I arrived at a statue, where I started talking to a few people, and I gave a whole two-hour seminar to about fifteen people in the street at midnight at Glastonbury in front of this statue.

I had started talking to two or three of them, and some other people stopped and they started to listen, and in the end, I had this little group around me. In many ways, that *is* the teaching. It's not a big anything. It's not a rah-rah presentation; you don't have to pay $1,500 to get in. It's just a person talking about their life, and that is your teaching.

What can we teach people? All we can teach them is about our life experience, then they listen, or they don't listen, and even if they don't listen, it doesn't matter, because they've heard it, and one day, it may be appropriate to them.

The fact that they don't go out tomorrow and give up drugs and straighten up and get a job working for the insurance company doesn't matter, because maybe their destiny is to go that other way. We don't know what people's destiny is. A lot of people are too weak to do what we want. They're too weak to follow along; they've got to go an alternative path.

I suppose, then, the teacher is the one who doesn't know she has taught. The healers don't know they have healed. The master builder never realized he built anything. It's in the example that you offer people.

Some of the initiates are born to it. They had visions. I was talking to one and she told me that she had visions when she was literally in the cradle, like at nine and ten months old that she can remember, which I found extraordinary. I don't remember anything before I was about three or four, and only very small snippets of information at that.

I think some of the initiates are born to it, but then I think other initiates come to it, and I can think of one or two that I know who were not initiates and were never near initiate, but they went through a massive transformation. Or they went through a transformation threshold that I talked about earlier where you start to create this threshold for yourself, where you begin to let go of the old you, and then you go through the lessons, albeit some of them are painful. You realize you weren't grateful, you realize that you were so insulting to humanity, not necessarily in the way you talked to them, because you might have been involved in social niceties, but in your heart and your thoughts. You were so degrading and so insulting of people's efforts and other people. Some of these people have gone through the pain of the struggle.

And then a lot of the initiates are just born to it like they're connected, but anybody can become connected once they're not cluttered. Certain people I've met specifically at seminars pretend to be terribly spiritual, but they'll never make it. You just know they're too arrogant in their thing. Or they get carried away with the power trips. So it's a kundalini trip, and all that sort of stuff. They can't let go of the whole sexual power they want over other people, by wrapping sexuality into spirituality. Not that the two aren't together, of course. Our spirituality and our sexuality is joined, but not by making it into a power tool.

One of the most spiritual people that I know, in the whole world, one of the really, truly great initiates is in jail at the moment for being a criminal. I would consider him one of the really, truly sacred beings. So you wonder how an initiate could be a criminal or in jail or dysfunctional. Or if they don't understand dysfunction, how could they be an initiate? If you hadn't done drugs, how would you understand heroin? If you hadn't been involved in all the human experiences that they are able to be in, how could you understand your humanity? You can't.

Consider that the person who is truly holy and good and dressed in their white suit and all that stuff—no way that they could ever make it. It's only those people who have actually truly been homeless, or in the gutter, or experienced the ghetto or the drug world or death, war, life, disease, violence, criminality, dysfunction, alcoholism, whatever. Only those people could ever be initiates, because initiate means they have completed in the sense that they have joined all these pieces together.

I am not saying that people should commit crimes or become heroin addicts to understand it, but I am just saying that there are many mystical people who come from that world, and then again, there may be other initiates who are professors at a university teaching Latin, or a priest at a seminary who will one day probably walk out of that priesthood, but he has it, or a nun working in Africa with children may have it. Mystical healing is everywhere.

I am offering a few extreme examples to show that these qualities don't come from saintly behavior. It's just being in the crosshairs of the feminine yin and the masculine yang where those two lines cross. Those initiates have the power they can see. They have snippets of the remembering that average people don't have.

Great visionaries usually come from terrible dysfunction, and maybe it wasn't that they were particularly dysfunctional, but they came from a family where their father beat up their mother and their sister ran away and their kid joined a gang and the whole bloody thing was a nightmare. They got to see it firsthand and lived it. When they lived it and made it right and didn't judge, they went beyond it. You don't judge things personally; you don't put people down if you can possibly avoid it, and then you don't necessarily make it wrong.

The Rebirth of the Power of the Feminine

People talk of a divine order, and that is correct, but usually they refer to it in the context of closing a real estate deal, or finding a soul mate, and that might not be quite as correct. For all the spirit beings and gods I have encountered in the celestial worlds, I have never met one that knew anything about romance or the multiple listing service.

The divine we see down here is what is sometimes called Gaia. That is the concept that the planet has a mind, a super knowing like we all do. In other words, it is an evolving spirit like you and me. Gaia says it knows about itself and it knows how to correct and heal itself, and, so far as I can tell, the divine order is the healing of everything. It's where aberrations in the digital facts of mathematics, of reality are put back together again, rebalanced.

In effect, I would say Gaia is the long-term will of the feminine principle, the goddess, and once you become soft, and you enter into her soul, into her perception, you become part of the magic of her, and you realize that the divine plan is vast and feminine.

Once you join her, she talks to you, and she shows you her vision. I have seen and documented over 30,000 full-color visions in the last four years. Sometimes they come in at the rate of 150 a day, and I would say that most of them have been about the goddess and Gaia and dimensions and the rebalancing of the planet, and that is why I said softness and a gentle eye is the key to everything. What I find so fascinating is that key books and films are appearing at regular intervals to help us along, not just the *Matrix* film, which is almost all true, according to what's in the morph anyway, but books like *The Da Vinci Code* that looks into the ancient manuscripts to discover that Mary Magdalene was a disciple of Jesus. She was very close to him, and some believe she was his wife. Even if she wasn't his wife, she must have been a good mate of his, someone he trusted.

The arrival of the goddess is all part of the rebirth of the power of the feminine, giving her back her place in the Trinity. Father, Son, and Holy Mother makes good sense to me. Anyway, I figured this goddess thing out before the morph showed up, so I went to Ireland to look for the Lady of the Lake. Because it says in the myth that she carried the wounded men across the lake through the mist to Avalon, I already knew that the myth wasn't a myth. It was real. By then I had seen the door even though I hadn't been through it yet.

If the door is real, then Camelot is real, the two are connected. So making peace with the feminine seems good tactics, especially for a young lad that didn't know if he was Arthur or Martha. I didn't have a clue at the time; I was about as green as a bunch of zucchinis. By the lake, I had a near-death experience. That was a bit spooky. I thought I was a goner, ever so slightly dead. I was hovering over my body at about six to ten feet in the air, but that was not what I planned. Then, after a few minutes of the out-of-body experience, I couldn't really find my body at all, and I went a bit blind, and that's when I got very scared.

There was a lad there; we called him the boy angel. He was a gypsy traveler. He was very soft and kind. I mentioned to him that I couldn't find my body, and he told me that I had been blinded by importance. I had an inkling he was right, but I was far too terrified and confused to get into the finer points of transpersonal psychology. So I just followed the lad's lilting voice, and it led me gradually to the water's edge. There, he kindly helped me wash my face, and I came back to Earth.

Life never looked the same after that. I saw the divine plan, and eventually I saw the queen and the grail, but I wasn't allowed to keep it. I had to go on a long journey through my stored pain as the boy angel had done.

I learned at the lake that all masculine things are up, the ego is up, intellectual ideas are up, money is up, competitive sports is up, war is up. Politics and control is up; the media are big liars, and they sustain up as holy and good. But if there is a God, if she's feminine, in the sense that the grace of creation is feminine, and that is why I think God is not a person necessarily, but the splendor of the God force in all things, the colors, the spark, the aliveness, the symmetry. It's her we are inside. The God is the Lady of the Lake, and she is vast, bigger than the entire universe.

We are in her in the sense that the balance of Gaia is in the master plan. It is the divine order, and if we are going to go toward balance in the feminine, we are traveling inside the planet, inside a divine order, and if we are in the masculine, we may well be ever so slightly dead, not built to last anyway.

After the lake, I made a shrine to the feminine spirit, that goddess in my heart, and perhaps you should also build a little shrine in your house, if the idea is not too weird and uncomfortable. It's good to hedge your bets. There's no evidence in the morph beyond the door, or in the celestial worlds, or in the factual worlds, for God the Father, or any male god. None. That may be hard for you to get your head around, but I wouldn't lie to you. What would be the point?

Instead, there's a mass of evidence for the feminine, not necessarily a goddess in human form, like Shiva or Kaali. I can't vouch for that but for the feminine principle. Now the Bible says the female came from the rib of the male, but what if it's backward and the male came from her rib? What if men think they are running the Earth, but, in fact, the feminine spirit is actually running the show? She's definitely in charge.

Now, you may ask, how does this give me defined benefits? And I would say, in all honesty, it may not give you an instant benefit, and then it might make you very excited, because you can now turn and go the right way, no matter what, knowing that it may save you from an upcoming disaster. Do you see the world of yang may not have much further to go?

Thousands of visions in the morph deal with variations of themes that describe the unraveling of the system that men built. The entire Western system may eventually fall apart. Maybe the planet can't handle the frenetic activity or any more activity. All activities are yang; sitting still is yin. Consumption is yang; conservation is yin. Maybe the morph arrived when it did because it is here to preside over the changes, to watch over us as humanity finally sees the answer, and they start to go the other way.

As I said before, the plan is vast and very soft and subtle, beyond anything we can understand, but if you spend time in silence, you will see the plan, and more importantly, you will see your part in the plan. You will hear the buzz that I talked of, and you will experience the downloads as you become more and more aligned. At the same time, you have to embrace the feminine and make her important. You should relax and wait and trust and realize the feminine is not a woman's version of masculine ideas and his lifestyle where she accommodates his ideas to become a sporty pushy type like him. That's the wrong way.

Many modern women think they are feminine because they have feminine parts and they are putting out a glamorous mask to show those parts off to their best avail, but often they are as masculine and as pushy as the men. Feminine is not anything to do with your parts; it's all to do with the quality of your imprint—snowflake or hellish. Just as Professor Emoto's crystals are hellish if you put the word *Hitler* on them, or beautiful if you put the word *Joy* on them.

The trick is to become less active, less male, and softer, and to become like an unseen current that flows deep underwater. By being patient and knowing, it's all going in the right direction, you join the plan, you *are* the plan. Struggling against the plan is just a recipe for more stored pain.

In other words, there's very little that you have to do. Just go the other way, and, remember, raising your energy is the act of getting rid of stuff (your husband maybe, just kidding). Mainly you have to simplify your life and not do less of what you have been doing because a lot of that hurt you badly, and I'm sorry about that.

Some may find this goddess concept hard to understand. It's a backward thing. The secret to everything is embracing the feminine, not just because she may eat you if you don't, but because it will carry you along if you do, and there is where you'll find the defined benefit. Trust me, I've been there, done that, lost my T-shirt, lost my body, lost everything, but I liked it in the end. If you handle your stored pain, and if you go through the three liberations and you truly go past the need to carry your story like a cross, then you become very free and more and more simple.

That is hugely inspirational to other people, and they will be drawn to you in droves. You'll be the only person in the neighborhood who is not spiritually crumpled like a pickled walnut. Complete strangers will start to tell you their life story at the supermarket, and you can become the magical healer. While you're getting used to that role, you can tell them what you think, but in the end, you will know that holding their hand is probably all that they will ever need.

The Arrogance of Consumption

Let me whizz through some of the feminine ideas, and maybe you can put some of the headings down in your dream journal that I mentioned earlier. You can watch and see if the feminine spirit starts to talk to you through your dreams and visions. It's cool if you start to talk to her and imagine getting into a permanent relationship. She's the one, trust me. You need alkaline, not acid. Acidity in your body causes disease.

Go for alkaline foods and alkaline surroundings, soft furnishing, and soft colors. The fastest way to change the pH factor in your blood is a squeeze of lemon juice and clean water. You think lemon is really acid, but lemon goes to very high alkalinity in your blood. Every meal you eat kills you a little bit more. Research shows that mice that have a very restricted calorie intake live 15 percent longer than mice that chow down at the regular rate. Less food is alkaline; more food is acid. Most vegetarian diets are very alkaline, especially raw food diets, but if you eat meat, fine. Just eat less of it and go for low-fat dairy products.

You need balance in your life, less activity, more silence, more soft music, less heavy rock and gangster rap, more softness and warm sentiments, and less confrontation and less stress.

Most stress is unnecessary. It's just you fighting to establish or sustain your ego's opinion as to what is supposed to happen, or it's conforming to someone else's demands. Maybe you can change that and be more free. Cities are acid; forests are alkaline as is the water in the mountains. You need less thinking, more feeling. Don't bother to work it out. The divine plan doesn't ask you to follow any logic that we understand anyway. Just keep asking yourself in every situation, *How does it feel?* Bag thinking, it's for amateurs.

Next go to neutrality as much as possible. Benevolence is feminine; antagonism is masculine. At best, if you can't manage benevolence, than be less insistent on your opinions. They're probably a load of rubbish that you've heard someplace. Don't be combative. There's no need. Let others go first. Let them win. Let them talk. Silence is feminine; noise is not feminine. If people have a need to be right, let them be right. Tell them, "Hey, brother, you're right," even if they're wrong. If they want to fight, walk away, be noncombative. It's safer, more spiritual.

Live and let live; adore everyone and especially praise your tormentors. They're teaching you things and what they're teaching is to go the other way. Be humble; you can never get enough of humility. It's the alkaline version of your soul.

You never really need to push yourself up or boast or struggle to get over people. To be one better, agree to be one less. Step to the back of the line. If you're balanced, you won't be in a rush anyway. Embrace everyone and exclude no one. That doesn't mean you have to carry home everyone you meet and feed them and so forth, but it does mean don't knock them down or knock them back. Instead, build them up, encourage them. Make them right, even if they seem to be acting a bit weird.

Be grateful and appreciative, not so demanding, and when I say appreciative, I don't mean a passing nod. I mean, really try to feel it in your heart, to feel the blessing of the people that you know, the gift of them so to speak, to feel the joy of the things you receive, to genuinely be appreciative for every small mercy. I'm always so shocked how people have so little gratitude and appreciation for life and the things that they are given. It's the arrogance of ignorance once more.

Listen, it's a bloody miracle you survived the night. Anything could have happened, and isn't it bloody marvelous that you're still here, and that you have a few friends and relatives that love you in spite of who you are, and how you might have treated them? Be grateful, and show it and mean it and say it and, more importantly, act it from your heart. Being grateful is feminine, while demanding the world provide and support you is masculine.

If you're not rich, then give of yourself. Offer a warm word and a kind sentiment and a helping hand. Give of your energy. Care for everyone. Giving not taking, remember, saving not using, trying to watch what you consume, and you start to consume less and less.

Action Step: Think about this. Get a small bag of rice and pour out the rice into seven cups. Not into big coffee mugs, just regular-sized teacups, and buy three onions and cut them into six halves. Next week, boil one cup of rice each day and eat that with half an onion. That's it, nothing else. Of course, on the seventh day, you won't have half an onion, and that's the point. There won't be any left. It reminds you how utterly wonderful onions are.

By the end of the week, you will learn to consume less and less, and you'll be so happy for all the varied food you shoveled in and passed out in his life. It was mostly an arrogance of consumption; you didn't need the half of it. The purpose of the Stuart Wilde Rice Week is so you see it for what it is, and you learn to be grateful for even a small cup of rice and half an onion. *It was good*, you'll say about the rice and onion week.

Now if you have health problems, or you're likely to suffer from this rice and onion method, then you should consult your health practitioner as they say in American TV ads. If you're not able to try the rice week, then turn off the TV for a week. Or try a full day of complete silence. Deprive yourself of something you like, like going around in your car. Take the bus for a week, or walk for a week, and then become aware of how grateful you are for having it all in your life.

Finally, being is better than doing, as it's in the quiet time that you feel the impulses I talked about in the last chapter.

Feel the Wobble of End Times

We are living in the strangest times that there have ever been. Because of TV, there's an external manifestation of the collective unconscious, in that we can see what others are thinking and doing, and we know what is happening in the minds of people all around the world. But what we're told by the news is not necessarily the truth. It's hard to realize how much the networks are massaging the stories. We have come to trust the broadcasts we see every night on TV. Yet the selling of the big lies is a manifestation in the construct of the matrix. It's the knots that hold the net together.

Each nation has a collective self, and you can see how deep within we are traveling at the speed of light further and further toward what is the edge of a cliff. You can see how governments are blind to reality. It's all about politics and donations and money and power trips. To put it more simply, humanity is collectively heading toward its global karma and the biggest crunch in history. You can already feel the wobble, and what you're feeling is the matrix cracking up. In other words, the guards of the matrix in the lobby of the hotel with the revolving door are starting to go ever so slightly mad, and they're losing control over the guests prancing up and down in ladies' tights doing the "Funky Chicken." The system is breaking.

Here's how it will help you. Develop the feeling of grace and deliver its redemption, gratitude, and service, and, of course, your humility.

You don't need to head for the hills and buy dry food. You could hide in downtown Detroit. You are a universe unto yourself. If you're an ugly universe, you will be aligned to the negativity and darkness, and they will eventually come and claim you if they can; but if you've turned to beauty, even a little, if you've gone from cold to warm and become a real human, then you can have your own mini Camelot, in your front room, if you want to. The door that I've spoken of in the past is right here. Put your arm out and look at the ends of your fingers. That is where the other world begins. It's the gap in the ceiling of the gymnasium where you can hide.

When the Twin Towers fell in New York, that was a big symbol of the start. They represented the peak of commerce and yang power, and they were very much a symbol of a global power force, a secret one, and our collective karma, the global madness within, brought them down. It was all part of the plan, and the plan is to bring us down, not up. It leads me to think that we're living inside a renewal, not the end of the world necessarily, but maybe the end of the world as we know it. But the end must include also a beautiful spiritual resolution for you and for me, and for all of humanity. It must come with forgiveness, not vengeance, with goodness and love, not condemnation.

I am often asked, *What is the nature of these end times*? And in the two versions of the end times, there's this sort of Armageddon scenario where the whole world possibly blows itself up in a nuclear confrontation; but then there's the second version of Armageddon, which is not violent at all, which just speaks of a spiritual revolution, the birth of the feminine, and, more than anything else, the acceptance of feminine ideals.

We don't know if the Armageddon is a literal Armageddon, or whether it's just a spiritual revolution, but there will come a time for sure, where the planetary ivory tower collapses, big time. So you could see a lot of businesses going broke, and the stock market falling apart, and you can see a lot of anger and pain. In the sense that we seek safety, it's not an exodus in the desert and running away from the Egyptians or something. It's more a safety where you retreat inside communities that are soft, or you retreat inside your heart. It's in your empathy that you arrive at safety.

Yes, the spiritual transformation began with New Age and with meditation groups, and with some of these Christian churches that are very forward looking—the alternative Christian churches that teach that sort of spirituality. The revolution is definitely here. It's coming, and it's coming very slowly, one step at a time.

The aftermath beyond the collapse of the ivory tower is a peace; it's a place where smaller communities band together to help each other, where there's less consumption and more interaction, more empathy. There's a place where real gratitude will come in where lettuce will seem like an incredible gift, and you think about lettuce where we are used to going into the supermarket and seeing thousands of lettuces of every kind, flowing in at unbelievable expense from the four corners of the earth. Kiwi fruits and various exotic foods and lemons that have been sent overnight express from Israel or South Africa, wherever they have come from. I mean, in the end, a lemon will be so valuable in your feelings. It becomes a part of your soul. You see that lemon, and you will be waiting for weeks for it to ripen, because you haven't tasted the lemon in months.

Some intuitives and psychics will say that they don't want to tell you that you have cancer because it's possible that in three years' time you will have healed by then or it's possible that your destiny won't go in the direction that they see it going. It's the same with our planet. It doesn't have to go where it's going, but consider the collected mathematics of our planet. The whole of this universe is just a mathematical formula, a fractal design, a geometry, which explains everything. It explains the mathematics of the binary system in our body.

If you tap your hand, the back of your hand, it sends signals to your brain according to a very defined on/off mathematics. It's not arbitrary at all, so the destiny of the world may be arbitrary, and it may not be arbitrary, but the destiny of the world is to change. It has to because if we continue on, with six billion people, eight billion people, everybody has a car, everybody's hurtling along, this whole planet just can't take the pollution, it can't take the activity, and it can't take the nastiness that will occur when resources become scarce. We have to ameliorate that by bringing back consumption.

One Armageddon scenario sees the whole planet wiping out with a few survivors only, and another scenario sees people beginning to learn to do things differently. I mean, imagine if every person who had a car drove ten miles a week fewer. That in itself would create billions of barrels of oil over a decade that we don't need to pump and put up into the atmosphere. It's more than likely an adjustment; whether it's a major adjustment or a minor adjustment, I am not in a position to say.

Your plan ought to include scaling back and getting smaller. There's no need to rush or panic, but bit by bit, as you can manage it, and if you can make money and forge ahead safely, then do so, but you should try to look at overall safety. Those who are highly leveraged may find themselves on the beach when the tsunami sea retreats.

Next, start to look and see how you might invest in yourself. Gain knowledge or a skill or some way that you will deliver service to humanity, as that is your plank for going sideways, if you can manage it, and see how much of your life is real and true and uplifting, and how much is a bit phony and debilitating. Then do this: Call to the celestial energies to retrieve you, call every night for a few minutes before you go to sleep. Let them know that you need to know, that you need to see that you are ready and willing to jump or act if you have to. Mobility will help you a lot. You have to become fluid in your feelings. That is what liberation is all about.

Today, you decide if you want the spiritual path. Or will you dither and waver and do nothing and pretend? Will you jump? If you jump, spirits come with a new grace to catch you, but you have to jump first without knowing if you will break every bone in your body at the bottom. If you let go and you trust, you will always be okay. It's only when you hang on that you miss your opportunities, and it hurts you a whole lot. It's a renewal, like the renewal the world is about to go through.

You learn to stay calm and don't panic, and you learn to let go and allow the forces to carry you. They know you don't know. I don't know. In a way you don't need to know because maybe if you knew, you would stuff it up and change your destiny. If you have embraced the feminine and the softness, you will have little resistance. Women don't resist the way men resist. They have a much greater ability to withstand pain than men. They are more allowing and passive.

In the softness, there will always be someone to love you and care for you because you will be in the kingdom of God where the hearts of people dwell. It's only in the yang world of creditors and hardness that you will be shunned, that people may walk over you in the street. Trust. Spirit is soft. Come.

The Mathematics of the Universe

In the ancient texts, the magical healer was given the number 22, and the master builder was given the number 11. He was the one that knew all about the sacred geometry and the mathematics of the golden mean, which is the spiral geometry that the Great Pyramid was built around. It was said that the master builder would rebuild the temple that was destroyed in Jerusalem, but I don't think it was meant literally. It's more that the master builder can hold the sacred space for people during the renewal and create a safe place for them to live and evolve a goal-free domain, and he or she had a rod with which to make proper measurements, and that rod was considered sacred, as it was precisely linked to the circumference of the earth and to the distance to the moon.

In other words, the master builder had a heavenly perspective, and he or she understood we live in a vast geometry where everything is interlinked.

Remember, I told you about rebirth in the void. You are the universe, it is inside you, and you are inside it. It is minute and vast at the same time, and you are minute and vast. You could hold the whole world in your heart. Once you allow your heart to expand, you could keep a thousand people safe and ten thousand beyond that, if you had the goodness and the willingness to do so. Someone will have to do it. That might be your final gift before you decide to leave—the gift of the master builder or call it the sacred mother who holds you safe in troubled times.

If you could manage that, it might be more than you ever expected in this lifetime. Nothing is impossible, once you can see your way. You can't believe what's coming for you, if you can accept it all and get ready. Perhaps you can use your resources to establish something really fantastic. Build something or make something available, create a center or a place—even a tent in a forest—where people meet and gather and talk about their lives, a place of safety. The world of the master builder energy is specialized, but there is a great need for them now to step up and get going.

The initiate was given the number 33. It's sacred in the mathematics of the divine plan, but the initiate was much more mysterious than the master builder or the magical healer. Sometimes he or she is the shaman that has the power of the nature kingdoms, and the doorways, and they know the herbs and the plant medicines; and then sometimes, the initiate is even more secret, and she or he moves the overall imprint inside the matrix without the ghouls or the dark energies knowing.

What I found so strange was that almost all of the initiates don't know they are what they are, and yet there are so many more of them than you would imagine, and all of them are very anonymous, not famous or obvious. I suppose their main function is to carry people across the gap, because there is a little gap between here and over there. Some are set in quite a military context. He or she can save people on the one hand and cause a bit of damage as well. Some of them have the power of the light and dark, and some live as if straddled between here and there in a transdimensional world where there is a constant battle going on between the forces of darkness and the forces of light.

If you are a part of the 33, I imagine you would have had an inkling of it for a long time now. Whatever you have been waiting for is now almost here. This will become your time over the next few years. What it will mean I can't say accurately, as the plan is so vast. It's well beyond me. I only know my little bit, and that is not very significant, but some of the initiates are commanders of vast armies. It's all in the morph, but there's a massive tussle going on to rob the ghouls of their power base and so bring the tyrants of this world to their knees.

Goodness knows how long. It takes many years I should imagine, but if you are drawn to the initiates' world, then you must be special. Inside you is a formula. You would have the knowing more than anything I could tell you, and you would have seen bits of the plan, your bits, the bits that are particular to you, and you would have seen them in your dreams and your visions.

Maybe you didn't believe them. Maybe you were waiting for someone to carry you out of where you are, but there's no one coming. You are the lifeboat because your energy is higher than anyone else's. If you don't know, no one knows, and all I would say is now is the time. Be brave. Make your move.

We have seen the mark on the forehead mentioned in Revelation. It looks like a vortex of energy that morphs and moves just under the hairline. In some people it's like a little donut. In others, it's like a spiral galaxy. The people with the mark are very important. They are the initiates, as far as I can work out. Yet the mark is hidden. You can't see it normally. I have only ever seen it on five people, but the power of the 33 will come into its own soon, and as it was told, at the very end, initiates appear and take people to safety. I think some people are born initiates and some people become initiates over a period of their lives. The downloads teach them, like the formatting sound that I mentioned in a previous chapter.

Then the number 44 was a scientific Christ consciousness. The eternal love of that is beyond good and evil, beyond the pain, beyond human life. I don't think we can know much about the 44. It's beyond the side door.

There's no 55 as far as I know and then 66 is the devil, which, of course, is not really a devil, just ancient stored pain. It's very interesting to me that if you add up the numbers of the master builder and the magical healer and the initiate together, they make 66, and if you add up the Christ consciousness and the magical healer, it also adds to 66.

Then after 66, there is number 77. As far as we know, it only comes once every 10,000 to 15,000 years. It is part of the renewal. It's not a person, but a fluctuation in the stability of the quantum vacuum of the universe. The only way I know how to describe it is to say it is a burst of light that comes out of nowhere, like spontaneous light that appears suddenly.

I don't know if you have ever tracked some of the UFO sites on the internet, but there's a whole lot going on right now about orbs of light, which I don't think are UFOs at all. I think they are lights in the morph. As some of the orbs are very geometric looking, they have a nice symmetry, which means they are probably not UFOs. I think they are part of the 77—balls of light that are part of the forces of light. I am not sure, and I wouldn't stick my neck out on this one, but we have seen the 77 in the morph. Strangely, we have seen it as a little box with angel wings.

It's more powerful than anything that has ever been here before. I think it is a synapse that takes place when the two worlds meet—the celestial world and this 3-D world. Maybe it's the day when you shake hands with your mirror self.

Where will it carry us? Out and beyond to a safe place, beyond the pain to a special place, what I call the *pain-free zone*. It may take us a while to get there, but there is never a rush. Take your time as fast or as slowly as you like.

Continue Your Journey Beyond Enlightenment

Here's something quirky to consider. Again, I have to go back to the *Matrix* film to explain it. Morpheus thought Neo was the One. The rest of the crew were unsure. The people at Zion thought Neo was the one. They worshipped him and begged him for favors and healing. Trinity believed in him and the Oracle wasn't sure. All the way through, Neo doesn't believe he is the one. Then at the end of the trilogy, he realizes he is the one. So he goes on the final journey into the heart of evil to save Zion and the human world, and then he fights the last battle with his little brother, the anti-Neo, the dark Mr. Smith, and, finally, in the film, he allows Mr. Smith to come into him and he embraces him. The very next thing is the light of the two joined beings, Neo and his opposite, make a burst of the 77. They burst to delight and Mr. Smith's program disintegrates into a thousand pieces. The dark explodes into light. The squeegees retreat and the human world of Zion is saved.

You are the one when you decide you are the one. Once you believe, you are the savior, not for everyone maybe, but to some. You are the master builder or the initiate; you are anything you decide. That's the strange thing about this journey. There's no one above to point you out or select you. It's self-selection, a kind of anonymous self-selection, You decide without telling anyone.

It's the deliverance that is beyond enlightenment, which is just a personal experience. Deliverance is how to enlighten everyone, by taking him or her through the gap where enlightenment is irrelevant, beyond good and bad, beyond light and dark. Beyond any of the normal definitions.

Pick a number: 11, 22, 33. Find your little brother or sister, make them right, love them. Then embrace softness and the goddess and let go, and you will see the side door, the one that leads you to the bliss heaven I spoke of. Look for the gap, it's everywhere, and remember this: you are the light and the dark and that dark is beautiful, and you are beautiful.

Let's answer the question: Why are humans here? We are here basically to evolve beyond our nastiness, to evolve beyond our separation, to evolve beyond war and mayhem and lies and so on. I mean, it's really like a school, so our purpose is to learn, but what we know about the celestial worlds, you have to trust me on this one. I have been in there. I have been in lots of them. The celestial beings guard their worlds ferociously.

There was a time probably in the evolution of the earth many thousands or tens of thousands, even a million years ago, when there weren't any dark energies here. It was literally a Garden of Eden, it was heaven, but bit by bit, dark energies began to infiltrate and take over this planet; they are inside the minds of the politicians. They are inside the military-industrial complex. They are inside the media. They are inside the lives that are driving people toward a collective insanity.

This has become the domain of the dark energies, the domain of the ghouls, and the goddess energy is basically here to get us back to rescue us from these influences. Most people don't realize that everything they do is impeded by some force somewhere, especially if they are trying to do something good.

Try doing something good and there will be a lot of impediments, and there will be people who will come in and try to stop you and impede you and hold you back, and there are others that will literally attack you because you are trying to do something good. Or they will decry what you are doing, or they will put you down or criticize you.

We have always got this impediment of the fact that the forces of control are up ahead of us on the path, and we learn to not fight those forces of control or not to fight the darkness, but to embrace it. We are learning a lesson, and the lesson is that we have to somehow integrate all these various aspects of ourselves such as how to be a father, and be disciplined, and have an authority over our children so they don't become maniacs, and keep them safe, and so on, yet teach them how to be soft. You know how to be a soft mother and still a good strong person who can teach your children. You know how to be a kind and loving boss and still turn a profit. It's all of those lessons; it's all the lessons of balance.

You are not here to be perfect. Don't beat up on yourself; love and accept yourself. Forgive yourself and love and accept others and forgive them. They are weak and imperfect, understand that. Care for them anyway. Realize, you are on a journey that has great honor, and great power, a journey beyond enlightenment—one that is infinite, and one that will carry you through your nostalgia for eternity to a higher plane.

As your energy goes up, bit by bit, all the sadness and the grief and the sense of futility and loss falls away, and you will reclaim your soul; you will remember, and that is what this journey is all about—remembering who you are and where you came from.

All of us humans came from a magnificent place, beyond pain and struggle. That place has a bliss that is so powerful, we had to move away for a while to recognize our soul, but once you do that, you will naturally return, for there is a celestial heaven forming right here on Earth, and you and I, in our terrible frailty, we both belong to that celestial heaven. One day when we finish sorting out a few bits and bobs, we will return. It's our destiny to return.

In our mother's pain, we were born, and through pain we did learn, and the law has decreed through love, we will return and that is so. That remembering I speak of comes softly to you from a very ancient place, a place that probably existed even before this universe was formed, and when you are soft and still and kind, when you understand a bit better, you will hear its whisper calling to you from a long way off. You will rise up because you are brave, and you will walk toward it. You have a right, for deep within there is a part of us that never left that celestial place and its ancient remembering. It is our divine right one day, finally, to go home.

About the Author

Thought to be one of the most renowned metaphysical teachers, Stuart Wilde described the etheric life field around humans in precise detail in the 1980s. Among his many teachings about love and peace were his revelations about spiritual evolution, personal development insights, philosophies about where human beings really came from, and predictions about world events yet to come that he would regularly see in transcendental meditation. Throughout the course of Wilde's life, hundreds of his predictions came true.

Wilde was born in England and educated at St. George's College, Weybridge, Surrey. He joined the English Stage Company in Sloane Square, London. And he opened a jeans business in Carnaby Street, London, during the heyday of the 1960s.

He studied alternative religions and Taoist philosophy. He immigrated to the US and lived in California.

In the 1990s he toured regularly with Deepak Chopra, Dr. Wayne Dyer, and Louise Hay, and lectured in New Thought churches and at New Age conferences.

He wrote more than twenty books—which were translated into twenty-seven languages and sold millions of copies worldwide—on the subjects of spirituality and personal development. He later executive produced and was the lyricist on popular New Age music albums.

In the course of his more than thirty years of teaching, Wilde appeared on hundreds of television shows and thousands of radio programs.

Wilde died in 2013 at the age of sixty-six. "Life was never meant to be a struggle; just a gentle progression from one point to another, much like walking through a valley on a sunny day," he said.

For more information: www.StuartWilde.com.

CPSIA information can be obtained
at www.ICGtesting.com
Printed in the USA
JSHW040429301122
34001JS00003B/3

9 781722 506025